MW01703357

Specific Skill Series for Language Arts

Paragraphs

Leveled Books in Nine Key Language Arts Skill Areas

SRA

Columbus, OH

The McGraw·Hill Companies

Cover: ©Tim Flach/Getty Images, Inc.

SRAonline.com

McGraw Hill SRA

Send all inquiries to:
SRA/McGraw-Hill
8787 Orion Place
Columbus, OH 43240-4027

Printed in the United States of America.

ISBN 0-07-601716-8

3 4 5 6 7 8 9 RHR 15 14 13 12 11 10

TO THE TEACHER

GENERAL INFORMATION ON PARAGRAPHS

Writers need to understand and apply the rules governing paragraphs in order to write effectively. A piece of writing with correct paragraphing helps the reader by breaking up long sections of prose and arranging ideas into more easily comprehended units. Writing strong paragraphs involves knowing that most paragraphs require a topic sentence and supporting sentences and that different types of paragraphs, such as narrative, descriptive, expository, and persuasive, have different purposes.

Common problems students have when writing paragraphs include the following:

- **Too short:** Paragraphs that contain only one to three normal sentences seem choppy and interruptive to the reader.
- **Too long:** Students who write overly long paragraphs might not understand the conventional structure of paragraphs.
- **Incoherence:** These paragraphs skip from idea to idea with no logical framework.

ABOUT *SPECIFIC SKILL SERIES FOR LANGUAGE ARTS*

Specific Skill Series for Language Arts is a companion to ***Specific Skill Series,*** a supplemental reading program that has been widely recognized for its effectiveness for over thirty years. The two series are designed and organized the same. ***Specific Skill Series for Language Arts*** consists of discrete units of practice exercises that target and reinforce fundamental language-arts skills. Units in both series are presented in multiple-choice format for standardized test practice.

ABOUT *PARAGRAPHS*

The scope and sequence for Books A through H of *Paragraphs* focuses on the purposes, planning, and structure of paragraphs. The scope and sequence for each book is located on the last page of the book. Each unit includes

- **rule boxes** that explain skills related to writing paragraphs.
- **models** in each rule box to illustrate the skills being discussed.
- **multiple-choice exercises** for skills practice and reinforcement.

Four **Language Activity Pages** (LAPs) appear in each book. Each LAP is divided into the following four sections and reviews the skills practiced in the preceding units:

Exercising Your Skill reviews key terms and concepts.

Expanding Your Skill provides mixed practice.

Exploring Language shows how the skills apply to real-world contexts by featuring one of six forms of writing: descriptive, narrative, personal, persuasive, expository, and poetry.

Expressing Yourself includes two creative activities related to the skills. One activity is always a Work-with-a-Partner activity to encourage collaborative learning.

TO THE TEACHER

SERIES COMPONENTS

- **Student Editions:** Nine books in each level (A–H) focus on nine skill areas: *Grammar, Usage, Mechanics, Spelling, Vocabulary, Sentences, Paragraphs, Writing Process,* and *Research.*
- **Placement Test Books:** One book for each skill area includes diagnostic tests to place students in the correct level.
- **Teacher's Manual:** Primarily an answer key, the *Teacher's Manual* also includes reproducible student worksheets and further information on how to use the program, including classroom management tips.

HOW TO USE *SPECIFIC SKILL SERIES FOR LANGUAGE ARTS*

Placing Students in Levels: The scope and sequence, complexity of skills, and readability in Levels A through H correspond to Grades 1 through 8. Students may, however, be placed in any level. For example, in the second grade, a student who needs remedial work in a specific skill may be placed in Book A, an on-level student who would benefit from skills reinforcement may be placed in Book B, and an advanced student who is ready for enrichment may be placed in Book C or higher. *Placement Tests* help place students in the correct level.

Setting: This series can be used for independent study and one-on-one practice sessions, as well as in small-group and whole-class settings. It is also effective in after-school and summer-school programs.

Getting Started: Students must have notebook paper or copies of reproducible student worksheets (located in the *Teacher's Manual*) before they begin working. Remind students not to write in the books. Students may begin in any unit of any book, depending on the skill practice they need, although it is recommended that they begin with Unit 1. As they work through the units, students should record their answers on notebook paper or on the student worksheets.

Pacing: Students should be encouraged to work at their own pace, completing a few units every day or every other day.

Scoring: Teachers should score units as soon as they have been completed. Then a discussion can be held in which students justify their answer choices.

Internet Use: Some activities, especially those in *Research,* require students to use the Internet. Students' use of the Internet should be monitored closely for content appropriateness and safety.

TO THE STUDENT

This book will show you how to write a paragraph. First, you will learn about three specific types of paragraphs: narrative, persuasive, and expository. Then you will learn specific ways to improve any type of paragraph you write.

In Book F *Paragraphs,* you will learn about

- Types of Paragraphs
- Paragraph Structure (Topic Sentence, Details, Closing Sentences)
- Improving Paragraphs (Staying on Topic, Transition Words)
- Writer's Craft (Figurative Language, Word Choice)

After you complete this book, you will understand the importance of staying on topic, paying attention to word choice, using transition words, and organizing your paragraphs effectively. You will also know that different types of paragraphs have different purposes. The purpose of a narrative paragraph is to tell part of a story, whether it is fiction or nonfiction. The narrative paragraph below begins with a description to set the scene, and it ends with the topic sentence.

Just inside the tall, blue gate, dreams became reality. Festive music from the merry-go-round filled the air as brightly painted horses cranked up and down in an endless circle. Carts suspended from cable carried excited visitors off to exotic lands with roller coasters and water rides. Fuzzy stuffed animals hung in the frames of arcade booths, where cheery young workers called out "Step right up!" Along the main thoroughfare, fountains of water rose high into the air, spraying parkgoers as they strolled by. My family's annual trip to Fun Town had arrived, and my brother and I were determined to ride every ride and see every show.

DETAILS

TOPIC SENTENCE

As you master the skills in this book, you will understand the structure of a paragraph and recognize the elements that are necessary for writing an effective paragraph.

Unit 1
Narrative Paragraphs

Topic Sentences

A **paragraph** is a group of related sentences that tell about a specific topic. When the purpose of the paragraph is to tell all or part of a story, whether fiction or nonfiction, it is called a **narrative paragraph.** Some narrative paragraphs move the story along by telling events as they occur in time. Other narrative paragraphs will contain a sentence that clearly states the paragraph's main idea. This type of sentence is called a **topic sentence.**

Most topic sentences come at the beginning of the paragraph. However, when the topic sentence asks a question, tells an interesting fact, or asks the reader to imagine something, the topic sentence may come later in the paragraph.

Read each paragraph. Then choose the underlined sentence that is the topic sentence. If there is no topic sentence, choose *None.*

1. **(A)** When Milton Hershey first went into the chocolate-making business, he planned and built not only a factory, but also an entire town surrounding it. For the families of his workers, Hershey built houses located on streets with names such as Chocolate Avenue and Cocoa Avenue. **(B)** He also constructed a fire department, an electric company, a telephone company, and a water and sewer system. **(C)** In addition to furnishing his workers with necessary buildings such as shops and stores, Hershey also provided for their leisure time by building a zoo, an ice-skating rink, a museum, and a park.
(D) None

2. When Arthur saw the low stone wall surrounding the garden, he stopped running and took a few deep breaths. **(A)** He moved slowly toward the wall, to avoid snapping a twig or making any other slight noise. As he peeped over the wall, he could barely make out two men standing in the shadow of the house. **(B)** They seemed to be arguing in low voices. Arthur strained to hear what they were saying. **(C)** All of a sudden, Arthur sensed that someone was behind him in the darkness.
(D) None

3. **(A)** Once the group finally made it into the road, they knew they would find their way back. Everyone breathed a sigh of relief but was too exhausted to cheer. The three men had been walking for days. Monroe looked at the dense forest behind them and couldn't believe they had come this far. **(B)** They all decided to walk a little farther before resting. An hour later they decided to stop for the night and set up camp a short distance back from the road. **(C)** Theo made the fire while Ben prepared the last of their food. Monroe filled up his canteen at a nearby stream, thinking that it would be a long time before he would go on another hiking trip.
(D) None

4. **(A)** This is the story of how perfume is made. The creation of a perfume begins with plant material, which might be flowers, spices, wood, leaves, or a combination of these. **(B)** The plant material is mixed with a solvent such as ethanol or methanol. The mixture is heated and the solvent evaporates, leaving a waxy concentrate of the plant material called concrete. After alcohol is added to the concrete, the mixture is heated, and then chilled. **(C)** The remaining plant matter and wax are then removed, and the alcohol evaporates. The essence of the plant material's fragrance is all that remains.
(D) None

5. **(A)** I was born on July 9, 1988, in Tuscon, Arizona. My parents' names are Thomas and Julie Wilburn. I come from a very large family. **(B)** My father has three brothers and a sister, and each one of them has at least two or three kids of their own. Can you imagine how much fun we have when we get together for holidays and birthdays? There are so many birthdays, it's hard to remember them all! In my own family, I have two younger brothers, Daniel and John. **(C)** We get along pretty well, although there are occasional disagreements over whose turn it is to do the dishes.
(D) None

Unit 1

Narrative Paragraphs

Topic Sentences

A **topic sentence** tells the reader what the paragraph is about. When you are writing, a topic sentence can help keep your writing in focus.

Topic:	Exercising
Topic Sentence:	Exercising is a key component to achieving a lifetime of good health.

Which topic sentence best completes each narrative paragraph?

6. ______ After struggling for several minutes to mount my horse, I was finally sitting in the saddle. I awkwardly held the reins and gently pressed my feet into the horse's sides. The horse responded by lowering its head and grazing on the grass. No amount of my tugging on the reins could budge the horse's head. I wiped the sweat from my forehead as the image of a pleasant gallop across the fields disappeared from my mind.

(A) We have to read the book *Black Beauty* for class and write a report on what we think about it.

(B) My grandfather once raised horses on his farm.

(C) I recently discovered that riding a horse is not as easy as it appears to be.

---

7. ______ Mark Twain's real name was Samuel Clemens. He worked as a journeyman printer and piloted a riverboat before setting out on a career as a writer, lecturer, and journalist. Clemens is credited with changing the tone of American literature by writing in a relaxed, humorous fashion. This style struck a chord in his readers and in those who tried to emulate his style.

(A) Mark Twain was an important figure in the history of American literature.

(B) I enjoyed reading *Tom Sawyer* and recommend it to anyone who wants to read a good story.

(C) Some of Mark Twain's books have been banned from school libraries.

8. There once was an English aristocrat, John Montagu, the Fourth Earl of Sandwich, who liked to play games. It seems he had a problem, though. It is said that he didn't want to get his hands greasy when he ate while playing, so he came up with an idea that would eventually make its way to many other parts of the world. He asked for some meat to be placed in between two slices of bread. _____

(A) I don't like any sandwich that has onions or tomatoes on it.
(B) This is how the sandwich got its name.
(C) There are many different kinds of sandwiches that can be found all over the world.

---

9. _____ For more than five years, Arnold led American troops into one dangerous battle after another. Bravely storming over a British barricade in the battle of Montreal, he was seriously wounded when a cannonball struck his leg. Time after time, Arnold continued to risk his life for the American cause.

(A) Few people ever respect one who betrays his or her country.
(B) Although the name Benedict Arnold has become a synonym for "traitor," the real Benedict Arnold began his career as a military hero for the American patriots.
(C) There were many brave people who gave their lives for American freedom.

---

10. _____ Columbus's goal was to sail west from Spain until he reached Asia. His intention was to open up a sailing route from Europe to Asia so that valuable gold, spices, and gems could be more easily transported to Spain. Although many people had been living there before Columbus landed, he discovered quite by accident that two huge continents and numerous islands interfered with a westward journey by sea from Spain to Asia.

(A) Columbus Day is celebrated on the second Monday in October.
(B) It is strange to say that Christopher Columbus discovered America when Native Americans already had been living there for many years.
(C) Although Christopher Columbus is commonly thought of as a great explorer, he originally had no intention of discovering or exploring new lands.

Unit 2

Narrative Paragraphs

Staying on Topic

If a paragraph has a topic sentence, all of the supporting sentences should relate to the topic sentence. This is called **staying on topic.** A paragraph that stays on topic is focused, and its main idea is clear to the reader. A narrative paragraph may not have a topic sentence, but the sentences in each paragraph of a story should be related to the overall theme of the story.

Choose the sentence from each narrative paragraph that does *not* stay on topic.

1. Few things in the world were as exciting as the first time my dad and I baked a pizza. **(A)** Even before we sank our teeth into it, the aroma of herbs and freshly baked crust sent out an inviting signal. **(B)** The sight of sizzling pepperoni pieces nestled in a blanket of melted golden cheese as we pulled it out of the oven was irresistible. **(C)** Even better than the tempting smell and sight was the long-awaited moment when we actually tasted the pizza. **(D)** Burritos are sometimes okay for a quick snack too. All of our efforts were certainly rewarded. The warm combination of flavors was more than delicious—it was perfection. We were so proud of ourselves!

2. After many years, the king and queen finally had a son. They were overjoyed! In honor of the birth of the little prince, the king and queen held a great feast. **(A)** Their castle was made mostly out of brick and mortar. **(B)** They invited all the fairies of the wood to celebrate with them. **(C)** In their joy, however, the king and queen forgot to invite the old fairy named Gwethyn, who kept to herself in the shadow of a huge oak tree deep in the forest. **(D)** To fix this problem, the good king decided to venture out into the darkest region of the woods himself to personally invite Gwethyn.

3. The Wright brothers started out their famous careers by building kites and toy helicopters. Later they constructed their own printing press out of spare parts from junkyards and barns. **(A)** When they were young men, the brothers also opened a bicycle shop where they built and repaired bicycles. **(B)** My brother and I build model airplanes. **(C)** The success of the bicycle shop allowed the brothers to spend most of their time building airplanes. **(D)** The money they received supported them during their early years of experimenting.

Unit 2
Narrative Paragraphs

4. At last the day was finally here. After weeks and weeks of waiting, it was time. Barely able to contain my excitement, I put on my shoes and jacket and ran out to the car to wait for my parents. **(A)** You are probably wondering what I was waiting for, right? It was my first trip to the circus! **(B)** If someone is really interested in something, it's a good idea to do research on it to learn more about it. **(C)** The acrobats, clowns, daredevils, and animals were simply amazing. **(D)** The whole time I was there I tried to picture myself being catapulted through the air and flying on the trapeze bars. On the way home I told my dad that when I grow up, I am going to join the circus. He just looked at me and smiled.

---

5. There is no debating the fact that Benjamin Franklin was an important figure in American history. **(A)** Franklin was born in Boston in 1706 and worked as an apprentice at age twelve for his brother, a printer. **(B)** In 1729, Franklin became the official printer of money for the colony of Pennsylvania. **(C)** He began publishing *Poor Richard's Almanac,* as well as the *Pennsylvania Gazette,* one of the colonies' first newspapers. **(D)** I wonder what kinds of stories he liked to publish. By 1748, Franklin had become more interested in inventions and science than in publishing. He spent time in London representing Pennsylvania in its dispute with England. He returned to America in March 1775 with the threat of war looming on the horizon. He served on the Second Continental Congress and helped draft The Declaration of Independence. He died in Philadelphia in 1790.

---

6. **(A)** Space travel is an interesting topic. **(B)** The explorers stepped hesitantly out of the spaceship onto the dry land of Mars. **(C)** It was unlike anything that the crew had ever experienced. **(D)** All around was red sand, rocks, and, in the distance, a city skyline that looked slightly out of place on the red, rocky horizon. A small green being with large black eyes walked up to them, one of his four hands outstretched in greeting. Captain Sally Furlongos stepped forward to take the Martian's hand. This was the dawn of a new era in which Earthlings and Martians would combine their technology to explore the outer reaches of the universe—where none before had been able to go.

Unit 3

Narrative Paragraphs

Dialogue

Dialogue is the words that characters speak in a real or make-believe story. In narrative paragraphs, dialogue makes characters seem real and also makes writing more interesting.

- Whenever a different person begins to speak, a new paragraph begins.
- Use quotation marks and punctuation correctly. The punctuation marks, such as end marks and commas, go inside the quotation marks when the speaker tag comes after the quotation. When the speaker tag comes first, the comma goes outside the quotation marks.
- The dialogue that follows in the next paragraph should logically follow the dialogue from the previous paragraph. What the speakers say should sound like language that people actually use.
- Speaker tags come before or after the quotation. Include the name of the person who is speaking.

  "It's time to go," said Peter. He had been waiting for his friend Gino for the last ten minutes.

  Gino answered, "I'm almost ready."

Which new line of dialogue makes the most sense based on what was said just before it?

1. It was Libby's first day at her new school, and she was a little nervous. She was trying to find her homeroom, number 217, when she ran into Kumiko.

"You look lost. What are you trying to find?" asked Kumiko.

______

(A) "I was just, like, so totally shocked at what Todd said," answered Libby.
(B) "Yeah, can you tell me where room 217 is?" answered Libby.
(C) "Oh, sure! I don't mind if I do," answered Libby.

---

2. Upon recovering from her initial fright by the spider, Little Miss Muffett stood up straight and bravely walked back over to the tuffet, determined to reclaim her curds and whey. Just then, Miss Muffett saw the spider helping himself to a heaping mouthful of curd. "Oh no you *don't!*" she said, running toward the spider.

______

(A) "Hey! You weren't supposed to come back!" protested the spider.
(B) "Yes, this is indeed a tuffet," said the spider.
(C) "I have eight legs and an entire cluster of eyes," said the spider.

3. Sammy and Rachel were sitting in class one day, listening attentively to the teacher. All of a sudden, Sammy's stomach started rumbling, grumbling, and growling. He squirmed in his seat, trying to make it stop, but nothing worked. He had skipped breakfast that morning, and now he was sorry—and embarrassed. Sammy looked over at Rachel. "Uh, did you hear something?" he whispered.

_____

(A) "This is one of the most interesting books I've ever read in my entire life," said Rachel.

(B) "You can if you want to," said Rachel, "but I certainly wouldn't recommend it."

(C) "Wow! I couldn't tell if that was your stomach or mine. I'm so hungry!" said Rachel.

---

4. It was a cold, blustery day outside when Desmond saw Mrs. Vartucken struggling to carry an armload of groceries from her car to her house. He was on his way to Fred's, but he could tell his neighbor needed help. Although he was terribly excited to try out Fred's new video game, Desmond figured it could wait an extra couple of minutes. He walked up to Mrs. Vartucken and said, "May I give you a hand?"

_____

(A) "No matter which way you look at it, red and blue make purple," said Mrs. Vartucken.

(B) "Oh, thank you!" said Mrs. Vartucken. "There are two more bags in the trunk. Do you think you could bring them inside for me?"

(C) "I guess it's time to renew my driver's license," said Mrs. Vartucken. "I can't believe I almost forgot."

---

5. Glug the Slug was on his way to his favorite vegetable garden one bright blue sunny summer morning. He was excited because he had heard that the red pepper plant—the best, according to Glug—was in full bloom. However, it seemed Dale the Snail had beaten him to it. He sat atop the highest petal munching away on leaf after leaf of this particularly popular pepper plant. "Hey, what are you doing?" called Glug to Dale. "I was waiting all month to eat that! You can't do this to me!"

_____

(A) "Well, come on up here!" answered Dale in return. "There's plenty to go around for the both of us!"

(B) "I have a shell where I hide when danger threatens," said Dale in between mouthfuls of leaves.

(C) "I heard you were almost fish bait the other night," answered Dale.

Unit 3
Narrative Paragraphs

- The dialogue in a narrative paragraph does *not* always need a speaker tag if it is clear who is speaking.

  "Would you like to go see a movie this afternoon?" Mr. Cuthbert asked his son.

  "Sure!" replied Dave.

  "What do you want to see?"

  "I'm in the mood for a comedy. What about you?"

  However, if there are more than two people talking together, it is best to include speaker tags so it is clear who says what.
- In the speaker tag, use a variety of descriptive verbs instead of always using *said.* Try using different kinds of verbs, such as *whispered, shouted, stated, inquired, replied,* and *asked,* that best fit the situation and that show how the person would be talking or responding.

Which new line of dialogue makes the most sense based on what was said just before it?

6. Tina turned around to look at her bedroom one last time. She remembered all the time she had spent there—all the phone conversations with her friends and all the talks between she and her sister, Maria. Tina was going to miss it all, but she knew that more good times and memories were waiting at their new house. She'd make new friends at the school, and then she and Maria would have all kinds of things to talk about. "Tina," her father called gently from the doorway. "We'll be waiting for you in the car whenever you're ready."

   ______

   (A) "Okay, Dad. Sometimes it's just so hard to say goodbye to something you love so much."
   (B) "Dad, were there carrots in the stew that Mom made for dinner last night?"
   (C) "I think these scissors are too dull to cut even this thin paper."

---

7. It was a little past seven o'clock in the morning when I heard a commotion in the kitchen. It was strange to hear such a noise so early on a Saturday, so I decided to go downstairs and see what was going on. To my surprise, there were Mom and Dad hunched over a brand-new bike—the very same one I'd asked for for my birthday! Bike parts lay scattered all over the floor. It wasn't looking good.

   "Sven!" called Mom, turning around. "What are you doing up so early?"

   "Yeah, go back to bed before you ruin your surprise," added Dad.

   ______

   (A) "Have you seen the dictionary anywhere?" I screamed loudly.
   (B) "Oil and water do not mix well," I stated.
   (C) "It's too late for that!" I exclaimed. "Besides, I'm way too excited to go back to bed now. Can I help?"

8. Julio and Stacey walked into the animal shelter. They already knew what kind of puppy they were looking for before they even walked through the door—a black Labrador retriever. Stacey always wanted a black lab. However, when they saw the sad, hopeful faces on all the other dogs, their hearts melted. "I want to take them all home!" said Julio.

"I know. Me too," returned Stacey. "They all deserve to be in good homes. How are we supposed to pick just one?" They continued to walk down the hall until Julio found the one.

____

(A) "Hey, Stacey! Look here!"
(B) "I just can't do this!" screamed Julio at the top of his lungs.
(C) "Do you have a quarter I can borrow?"

---

9. Steve was in a hurry and ran out the front door without his lunch bag. Of course he didn't do it on purpose, but he heard the bus rumbling down the street and could think of nothing else but making sure he caught it. Today was the day of his science fair presentation, and he surely didn't want to be late. His mother noticed the brown sack he left on the counter and ran out the door after him. "Steve!" she called. "Hold on a minute; you forgot your lunch!" Steve spun around on his heels to go back and get it.

____

(A) "Thank you *very* much!" hissed Steve through clenched teeth.
(B) "Get out of my way!" yelled Steve.
(C) "Thanks, Mom. You're the best!" he said, stopping just long enough to grab the bag.

---

10. John, Chandler, and Becky were in the cafeteria eating lunch when their art teacher, Mr. Stickler, walked up to their table and asked if he could sit down. The three friends looked at each other, smiling and not sure what to expect. John nodded, and Mr. Stickler took the seat next to Chandler.

"Well, gang, how would you like to help me create the scenery for the school play? I know you're a creative bunch of people, and you'd be great at it. What do you say?" asked Mr. Stickler.

"That sounds interesting!" Becky stated, looking around at her friends.

____

(A) "I told my grandma I'd be home right after school today," whispered John to Becky.
(B) "Something must be done about the quality of this food, and you are just the person we need," said John.
(C) "Is there any particular set you had in mind, Mr. Stickler?" inquired John.

Unit 4

Narrative Paragraphs

Closing Sentences

A paragraph should include enough information to make your ideas clear. The last sentence in the paragraph is the **closing sentence.** Sometimes, the closing sentence repeats the main idea of the paragraph. Other times, the closing sentence gives a final thought or idea about the main topic, a summary of the paragraph, or a smooth transition into the next paragraph.

Which closing sentence best completes each narrative paragraph?

1. Everything has a history and comes from somewhere. Although you may not always think of something as common as a flashlight as having a history, it does. One of the first flashlights was invented in 1898 by a Russian immigrant in New York City. The inventor's first flashlights were made from paper and fiber tubes with a bulb and a rough brass reflector. Batteries were weaker back then, and bulbs were not as advanced as the ones we have today. ______

(A) Before you take your flashlight anywhere, make sure you have a supply of fresh batteries.

(B) Nobody ever wants to be caught in the dark without a flashlight.

(C) As a result, the flashlights back then produced only a brief flash of light, which is how they got their name.

2. In October 2003, China sent its first manned spacecraft into space. This was a milestone for the country because it is only the third country in the world, other than the former Soviet Union and the United States, to send a person into space. Astronaut Yang Liwei circled Earth about every ninety minutes aboard the *Shenzhou 5* spacecraft. He remained in orbit for about two days before reentering Earth's atmosphere and landing in China. ______

(A) Upon Mr. Liwei's safe return, he was regarded as a hero to many in his homeland.

(B) Earth's atmosphere is made of different layers.

(C) People were wondering if Mr. Liwei could see the Great Wall of China from space.

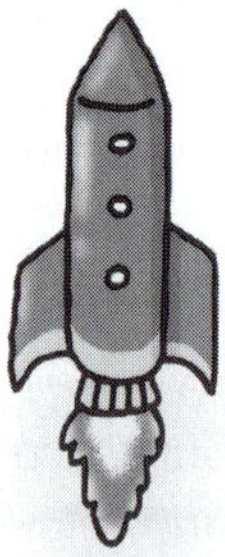

3. It's a well-known fact in this part of the kingdom that one should avoid Myronis's Reflecting Pool, which lies in the depths of the old forest. The rumor is that if you look into it and see Myronis's reflection, you have to complete a task for her; otherwise, she'll turn you into a frog. Only one who is pure in heart can gaze into the pool and see his or her own reflection, and when that happens, Myronis will grant the gazer one wish. To the best of everyone's knowledge, this has never happened. Many a traveler seeking to quench his or her thirst has unknowingly knelt down and gazed into the pool's sparkling waters only to see the twisted form of Myronis's face. ______

(A) The pool's water is too cold to swim in.

(B) They are never heard from or seen again.

(C) Someone should just drain that pool so nobody has to worry about it.

---

4. My grandpa lived an interesting life, and I have always admired him. In World War II, he drove an ammunitions truck and supplied ammo, weapons, and other necessities to soldiers. After the war he returned to Michigan and married my grandmother. They moved to a couple of different places before finally settling in California. By that time, my dad and Uncle Bernie had been born. Not long after that, Grandpa started his own business. He was very talented with his hands and loved to carve things out of wood, so he started making and selling guitars from his basement. He also began to write a book about his life. He never finished it in his lifetime, but Grandma gave it to me for my birthday last year. It is one of my most prized possessions. ______

(A) I am proud to be his grandson, and I hope I can be like him someday.

(B) My dad has two brothers and a sister who all live nearby.

(C) My mom's family is much smaller than my dad's family.

---

5. Born in 1871, Theodore Dreiser worked as a journalist in the Midwest, where he was born, and eventually settled in New York City. His first novel, *Sister Carrie,* published in 1900, drew on the city life he observed around him. Many people did not like the novel because of its subject matter, and to Dreiser's disappointment, the book received little exposure. In 1911 Dreiser published *Jennie Gerhardt.* Again he experienced censorship when others viewed his work as immoral. ______

(A) I wonder what Dreiser would think of the books that are censored today.

(B) Many other famous writers come from New York City.

(C) Despite these setbacks, Dreiser, who died in 1945, is credited with being a major American writer.

The First LAP

Language Activity Pages

A. Exercising Your Skill

You have been learning about writing topic sentences, staying on topic, and using dialogue associated with narrative writing. Answer these questions about what you have learned.

1. What does a topic sentence do?
   (A) brings a paragraph to a logical end
   (B) clearly states the paragraph's main idea
   (C) lets the reader know that there will be dialogue

2. What is one characteristic of a narrative paragraph?
   (A) it tells all or part of a story
   (B) it gives facts
   (C) it tries to get people to think or feel a certain way

3. When is it okay for a paragraph to have sentences that do *not* stay on the topic?
   (A) when the paragraph is running long
   (B) it is never okay for sentences to be off the topic
   (C) when a lot of ideas are introduced in a paragraph

4. What should dialogue be like in a narrative paragraph?
   (A) it should always be funny
   (B) it should be short and to the point
   (C) it should sound like language the characters would really use

5. What can the closing sentence of a paragraph do?
   (A) give a summary of the paragraph
   (B) introduce a new thought or idea
   (C) begin a new paragraph

B. Expanding Your Skill

Read the following paragraph. Choose the topic sentence that goes with it.

_____ After being disabled by an accident, he dedicated himself to creating written symbols for the Cherokee language. At first, Sequoya tried to create simple pictures to represent Cherokee words, but later he developed eighty-six symbols to represent all syllables in Cherokee speech. He then had his six-year-old daughter demonstrate his system of reading and writing to Cherokee leaders.

(A) Different Native American tribes did not all speak the same language.
(B) Learning to read is one of the most important things a person can do.
(C) Sequoya is remembered for inventing a written language for the Cherokee.

C. Exploring Language

Narrative Writing Read the following paragraph. Not all of the sentences belong in it. Number your paper from 1 to 4. Write the letter of each of the four sentences that do *not* stay on topic.

(A) We began our tour of New York City at Grand Central Station. (B) People travel all over the place on trains. (C) From there we walked all the way to Central Park because we were so excited to see it. (D) That was one of my favorite parts of the trip. (E) I loved climbing all over the big rocks. (F) Near a pond we stopped for a hot dog break. (G) I also went for a ride on the merry-go-round. (H) It's not uncommon to also find these kinds of rides at festivals or fairs. (I) Next we walked to a large toy store. (J) It was the biggest, most awesome toy store I have ever seen in my life! (K) Once kids reach a certain age, they don't get many toys after that. (L) However, my older brother is twenty-four years old, and he and his friends all still like to play video games, so who knows!

D. Expressing Yourself

Choose one of these activities. When you are finished, give your paper to your teacher.

1. Write a paragraph about a place you have visited recently or would like to visit. It may be a field trip or a real or an imaginary vacation. Tell a story about what you did there or about something that happened. Include dialogue that shows what the characters in your story are thinking and feeling. Remember to make the dialogue sound like language they would really use. Also write a topic sentence, and be sure to keep every sentence on the topic and end with a closing sentence.

2. WORK with a PARTNER Work with a partner to write a narrative paragraph. It may be a short story, or it may be one paragraph out of a larger story. You may even want to place yourselves in the story. Take turns writing one sentence each. It would be helpful to discuss what you will write about before you start writing. Include dialogue that represents the way the characters would actually speak, using appropriate speaker tags. Also make sure your sentences all stay on the topic.

Unit 5

Persuasive Paragraphs

Topic Sentences

A **persuasive paragraph** is a group of related sentences that make a claim, which is then supported by evidence. A **claim** is a statement that the writer makes and uses to try to persuade the audience. Your claim should be stated in the topic sentence. The topic sentence can appear near the beginning or at the end of the paragraph, depending on how you organize the paragraph.

- A good topic sentence for a persuasive paragraph will help introduce the topic and your feelings about it.

  Young children should spend more time reading than watching television.

Which topic sentence best completes each persuasive paragraph?

1. _____ However, most Americans could enjoy healthful and appetizing meals and snacks instead of the junk food that they enjoy too often. More than ever before, a wide variety of fresh fruit and vegetables and low-fat foods are readily available. When these foods are stocked at home, they are just as convenient as fast-food restaurants. More importantly, they are far more healthful. When you get the urge for a snack, try a kind of apple you've never tasted before or carrot sticks.

(A) There are different ways to prepare meals with fresh fruit and vegetables.
(B) The world is full of all kinds of food.
(C) In America today, it is common for people to ruin their health with a poor diet.

---

2. Eggs can be a central part of virtually any meal. For breakfast, eggs can be fried, poached, scrambled, or used to make omelets. Egg salad, pickled eggs, and deviled eggs add zest to any lunch. For dinner, eggs can be made into quiche or casseroles, or they can be used in a variety of sauces and soups. Eggs are also an essential ingredient of most desserts and baked goods. _____

(A) All of this information proves that eggs are an incredibly versatile food.
(B) Eggs are a good source of protein and vitamin B.
(C) You can use eggs as a substitute for meat.

3. Why should people bother to vote in national elections? After all, one vote doesn't make a difference—national elections are decided by a margin of tens of thousands of votes. Unfortunately, this view is held by many Americans—in fact, millions of Americans. If even a fraction of these citizens would take half an hour to vote on Election Day, they would change the outcome of many elections. Our country was founded on the idea of government for the people by the people. _____

(A) Our nation's voting system needs a major overhaul.
(B) Every citizen should value his or her right to vote and exercise it.
(C) There are many things that have made this country great.

---

4. Are you tired of wearing the same old clothes long before you are able to buy new ones? _____ Today's secondhand clothing shops buy and sell gently used and never-used clothing that is still in style. All you do is bring in clothes that you no longer wear and that are in good condition. If the person working at the shop thinks your clothes could be sold, he or she will pay you for them. Then you can use that money to buy the clothes you want. The clothes may not be exactly new, but they'll be new to you! Plus, you will be able to purchase some of the same clothes at the secondhand store that sell for a much higher price at department stores.

(A) If so, perhaps you should consider shopping at used clothing stores.
(B) If so, you are not alone in feeling this way.
(C) If so, there are some options for you to consider before you throw your old ones away.

---

5. _____ Doing so would reduce the amount of accidents on the roads. An article in the newspaper recently stated that drivers between the ages of sixteen to nineteen have the highest rate of involvement with fatal crashes. If a law was passed that required teenagers to wait to drive until they are at least twenty years old, there would be fewer accidents. The roads would be a much safer place to drive. Teenagers could spend that time learning how to be better drivers. The article also said that driving errors account for eighty percent of accidents involving teenagers. I am sure you will agree with me. Let the teenagers wait until they are really ready to take on such a responsibility.

(A) The speed limit on our highway should be raised to seventy-five miles per hour.
(B) Driving a car, a truck, or a motorcycle requires taking a lot of responsibility.
(C) I think the minimum age for obtaining a driver's license should be raised to twenty years old.

Unit 6

Persuasive Paragraphs

Order of Arguments

A persuasive paragraph makes a claim and supports the claim with arguments, or evidence. A **claim** is a position or viewpoint that the writer must prove by the use of arguments. An **argument** is a reason for or against an idea.

Claim: Brett Favre is the best quarterback of all time.

Argument That Supports the Claim: Brett Favre has led his team to many come-from-behind wins.

- A persuasive paragraph often includes several arguments to support the claim. These arguments can be organized from weakest to strongest so the last point leaves a lasting impression on the reader. Another strategy is to organize arguments from strongest to weakest so the most important argument grabs the reader's attention.

The arguments in each paragraph below are organized from weakest to strongest. Choose the argument that fits the claim and best completes each paragraph.

1. Installing vending machines in schools is a bad idea. _____ Second, students would be more likely to skip lunch and eat only the sugary, high-fat snacks from the machine. Lastly, studies show students do not perform as well in school when they don't eat healthful foods; most vending-machine snacks are not part of a healthful diet.

(A) The cafeteria already offers a variety of nutritious snacks that students can choose from if they do not like what is on the menu.

(B) The most popular snacks purchased by students are potato chips.

(C) Establishing a dress code is also a bad idea.

2. Our national parks are in need of attention and support. _____ In addition, recent brushfires that swept through Yosemite National Park and other western areas destroyed many acres of trees. Last, financial support for the parks from the federal government has dropped. Without that support, the parks cannot be maintained properly. National Parks are our heritage. We cannot afford to ignore them.

(A) National Parks have many swingsets and sandboxes available for young people to play in.

(B) One danger to parks is overcrowding, as each park attracts thousands of tourists each year.

(C) State parks are fun places to spend a weekend camping and fishing.

3. Our school needs a new basketball court. A newly paved basketball court with new nets would encourage more students to play basketball. The one we have now has so many cracks that it's practically impossible to play on it. If the ball hits a crack in just the right way, it goes flying off into another area of the playground. Also, none of the rims have nets anymore. The state of the school's basketball court is a poor reflection on our school. _____ We all know this isn't true because our school takes pride in everything it has and does.

(A) The basketball courts need new free throw, out-of-bounds, and three-point shot lines painted on the asphalt.

(B) The baseball diamonds are overrun with weeds, and the fences are damaged every time a thunderstorm comes.

(C) If visitors come to the school and see what the court looks like, they may think that this is how we take care of everything else.

---

4. Students should start learning how to speak a foreign language much earlier than high school. I have read that younger students are able to learn a new language much easier than when they are older. _____ Finally, with so many people immigrating to the United States who don't know English very well, it is important for us to be prepared to meet their needs, especially those of their children. Knowing how to communicate with them in their own language is one way.

(A) Linguistics is the study of the origins of language.

(B) Also, as opportunities to work overseas increase, knowing a second language would help make job seekers more qualified candidates.

(C) Spanish is the second most common language spoken in the United States.

Unit 6

Persuasive Paragraphs

The arguments in each paragraph below are organized from strongest to weakest. Choose the argument that fits the claim and best completes each paragraph.

5. Which class is the best of all? That's an easy question to answer. ____ This year we read stories by writers from as far away as Russia, Spain, England, and Africa. You can learn a lot about yourself and others by reading stories about people, even if they are fictional characters. Reading class gives you an opportunity to read all kinds of literature that you may not otherwise have ever heard of. Besides, it's just plain fun! Clearly, reading is the best class of all.

(A) Reading is the most interesting because we get to explore many different kinds of literature.

(B) In study hall, you will get the opportunity to study all of your subjects in a quiet environment.

(C) Mathematics is also a very important and interesting class.

---

6. Why should you participate in the school's annual fundraiser? ____ It also provides the school with extra money to save for other expenses, such as new books and desks. Besides, working together builds an atmosphere of cooperation and can build new friendships. It is important to participate in the fundraiser because it helps the school and you.

(A) Much of the money goes toward art and sports programs that the school wouldn't be able to support without the money raised by the fundraiser.

(B) Money comes from many sources, including federal grants and local property and income taxes.

(C) Money from the fundraiser will help fund a new trophy case for the front hallway.

---

7. Hitting home runs is much easier today than it was twenty-five years ago. First, new baseball diamonds are built much smaller than they used to be. Pitching in the major leagues is not as good or consistent as it was then because of how many teams there are in the league today. ____ Finally, the workout programs of baseball players are much more effective, and the players are bigger and stronger than they were in the 1970s.

(A) Johnny Bench was the greatest catcher of his generation.

(B) The 1976 Cincinnati Reds were a much better team than the New York Yankees of today, even though they hit many fewer home runs.

(C) Another reason why it is easier to hit home runs is because the baseball itself is constructed differently than it used to be.

Unit 6

Persuasive Paragraphs

8. Have you ever considered a career in art? Many people think that the only way for a person to succeed as an artist is to produce works of art, such as paintings and pottery. This is a misconception; there are virtually hundreds of careers in art. For example, there are creative opportunities for interior designers, fashion and jewelry designers, industrial designers, and toy designers. _____ You should consider being an artist because artists have a lot of fun in their line of work. They enjoy what they do—creating something out of nothing. There are many options available for people who wish to have a career in art.

(A) Jackson Pollock was a famous painter who invented a new way to create paintings.

(B) Other options include book illustrators, mapmakers, photographers, computer graphics artists, and Web site designers.

(C) Art is truly the greatest human invention, and everyone should participate in an artistic pursuit.

---

9. Would you like to do something that could help you grow physically, mentally, and socially? If so, you should try playing a sport. You can grow physically by playing a sport because you will be exercising your muscles every time you play. _____ You can also grow socially because, when playing as part of a team, you learn to work with people. Also, you can make new friends. Sports can be a lot of fun once you pick the one that is right for you. For example, if you like to run, try playing soccer or football. If you like fast-moving sports, try racquetball. The important thing is to find one you enjoy and stick with it. Sports truly help to make a well-rounded person.

(A) The heart is the most important muscle in your body, and it needs to be healthy and strong.

(B) Swimming is considered to be the best exercise for a person's entire body.

(C) You grow mentally because some sports, such as golf, require a lot of thinking.

Unit 6

Persuasive Paragraphs

Fact and Opinion

When writing and organizing the arguments in your persuasive paragraphs, it is important to know the difference between a fact and an opinion.

- A **fact** is something that is true without a doubt and can be proven through research.

  Not all birds are able to fly.

- An **opinion** is usually something that someone thinks or feels and is not always true.

  A vulture is the most beautiful bird in the world.

When you do any kind of persuasive writing, whether it is a paragraph or an entire paper, it's a good idea to rely mostly on facts to persuade your audience. Complete any research that is necessary to find facts that support your claim. Limit your use of opinions to those made by experts in the field you are writing about.

Which fact or opinion best supports each claim? If neither piece of evidence supports the claim, choose *Neither*.

10. **Claim:** Traveling by airplane is better than driving.
    Evidence: Traveling time is greatly reduced when flying in an airplane.
    Evidence: ______
    (A) My friend likes airplanes better because he thinks flying is more fun than driving.
    (B) Research shows there are more driving-related deaths yearly than there are airplane-related deaths.
    (C) Neither

11. **Claim:** Certain kinds of shoes can help a person run faster and jump higher.
    Evidence: Roger could jump much higher after buying the new Sky Hoppers shoes.
    Evidence: ______
    (A) Kyle says the thicker the sole of the shoe is, the faster you can run.
    (B) I think newer shoes can improve the performance of some athletes.
    (C) Neither

12. **Claim:** The Internet is a better source of news than a newspaper.
    Evidence: You can find information about all kinds of topics and issues on the Internet.
    Evidence: ______
    (A) The articles on many news-related Web sites are updated throughout the day; however, newspapers are printed only once a day.
    (B) Mom thinks the Internet is the best invention ever made.
    (C) Neither

13. **Claim:** Exercise and a balanced diet are the best ways to maintain optimum health.
Evidence: Research shows that diet pills produce only short-term benefits; weight is regained once the person stops using the pills.
Evidence: _____
(A) My doctor says the best way to stay in shape is to exercise daily and eat a well-balanced diet.
(B) My great-grandpa thinks that people would live longer if they slept more.
(C) Neither

---

14. **Claim:** Our city would be safer if it had a curfew for kids under eighteen years old.
Evidence: The streets would be safer because there would be fewer juveniles on the street late at night.
Evidence: _____
(A) My sister feels that a curfew would make our city safer, allowing more people to walk after dark.
(B) Reports show that crime levels drop when cities adopt some sort of curfew.
(C) Neither

---

15. **Claim:** Although suntans make you look nice, too much sun can severely damage your skin.
Evidence: Sun poisoning can result from overexposure to harmful ultraviolet rays from the sun.
Evidence: _____
(A) Studies have proven that you run the risk of getting skin cancer from staying unprotected in the sun for too long.
(B) I can stay out in the sun all day without getting too burnt.
(C) Neither

---

16. **Claim:** Classical music can be just as exciting as rap or rock-and-roll music.
Evidence: Some rock-and-roll musicians incorporate elements of classical music into their own compositions.
Evidence: _____
(A) Alonzo, a big fan of rap music, says he thinks some classical music is cool.
(B) Brian says he thinks his favorite band will use a string section on their next CD.
(C) Neither

Unit 7

Persuasive Paragraphs

Closing Sentences

The closing sentence at the end of a persuasive paragraph often appears in one of two different ways.

- One way is to restate your claim. Also, if you began your paragraph with a question and haven't stated your claim yet, you may state it here.

  As I have already suggested, a tarantula is no scarier than a teddy bear.

- Another way to close a persuasive paragraph is to suggest a plan of action. This method will only work when there is a realistic action that the reader can actually take.

  The next time you are out on a walk and see a piece of litter lying in the street, do not hesitate to pick it up and throw it away.

Which is the best closing sentence for each persuasive paragraph?

1. The next time you come upon a movie that you'd like to see, check whether it is based on a book. If so, read the book before you go to see the movie. Most people will tell you the book is usually better than the movie. Often, a book will let you see more deeply into a character. It will also give you a chance to use your imagination and creativity to imagine what the characters and setting look like. Then watch the movie, and compare it with the book. ______

   (A) You will see that, many times, the book is better than the movie version of the same story.

   (B) A movie without a strong soundtrack is a weak movie.

   (C) What if there is no book available of the movie?

2. Do you ever feel gloomy or get depressed? If you feel this way sometimes and don't know what to do about it, try doing a random act of kindness for someone else. That way, you can focus your energy on making another person happy instead of just thinking about your own problems. You may find that the smile you bring to the unsuspecting person's face could lift you out of your own bad mood. The world would be a better place to live if we all helped each other more. ______

   (A) Talking to a school guidance counselor is a good way to help you overcome a difficult situation.

   (B) You don't always have to keep your emotions bottled up inside.

   (C) So the next time you are feeling down, do something nice for a friend, a relative, or a stranger, and see what happens!

3. When you get thirsty on a hot summer day, what is the first thing you reach for to quench that thirst? It should be a glass of water. Water is an essential nutrient. It is necessary for maintaining body temperature, transporting nutrients throughout the body, keeping joints moist, digesting food, and cooling the body. Experts recommend that adults should consume about $2\frac{1}{2}$ quarts of water per day. Children should drink about half this much. Other drinks such as pop or soda should be avoided because they contain high amounts of sugar and caffeine that only make you thirstier. ______

(A) Sports drinks are not necessary unless you are involved in an extremely heavy workout routine.

(B) Clearly, a cold glass of water is the best and healthiest way to replenish your body's lost fluids.

(C) Caffeine speeds up your body's heart rate and respiration, which makes you lose even more water.

---

4. People should consider riding bikes to work when it's possible. There are several reasons for this. First, streets and highways would not be as crowded, thus reducing the risk of accidents. Second, there would be less harmful exhaust released into the air from cars, SUVs, and trucks. This would reduce the amount of air pollution. Third and finally, less oil and gasoline would be used, conserving more for future use. ______

(A) Some natural resources can never be renewed once they are totally consumed.

(B) Walking is also a more economically and environmentally safer solution than driving.

(C) So the next time you get ready to go somewhere, ask yourself if you could ride your bike instead of driving.

---

5. I think the cell phone ban in our school should definitely be lifted. They are important to have so we students can get in touch with our parents in the event of an emergency. There simply aren't enough public phones to accommodate everyone. If the cell phones were turned off during class, they wouldn't disrupt or annoy anybody. We could also limit cell phone use to before and after school. Another reason cell phones should be permitted in our school is that they are becoming a normal part of society and should be accepted as such. ______

(A) Cell phones are more a necessity than a convenience and, under certain conditions, should be permitted in our school.

(B) Do many people even carry pagers these days?

(C) Wireless technology, like many things in society, has its drawbacks and benefits.

The Second LAP
Language Activity Pages

A. Exercising Your Skill

You have been learning about parts of persuasive paragraphs, including topic sentences, order of arguments, facts versus opinions, and closing sentences. Answer these questions about what you have learned.

1. What does a persuasive paragraph do?
   (A) makes a claim, which is then supported by evidence with the intention to influence the reader to think or feel a certain way
   (B) tells a story
   (C) describes in detail how something feels, tastes, looks, smells, or sounds

2. Which of the following is an example of how arguments in a persuasive paragraph may be organized?
   (A) left to right **(B)** weakest to strongest **(C)** funniest to most serious

3. What is the difference between a fact and an opinion?
   (A) A fact is undoubtedly true and can be proven with research, while an opinion is what someone thinks or feels and that may be wrong.
   (B) A fact is based on something that someone says, while an opinion is a scientifically tested statement.
   (C) A fact should never be used in a persuasive paragraph, while any kind of opinion may be included.

4. What kind of opinion might you use in a persuasive paragraph?
   (A) a friend or a relative's opinion
   (B) any opinion that seems to support your claim
   (C) a quote from an expert in the field you are researching or writing about

B. Expanding Your Skill

Choose the topic sentence that belongs with the following paragraph.

_____ Vinyl records contain the sound that the musicians originally intended for listeners to hear. Many older classic albums are remastered by someone other than the original producer of the album or the band, and it just doesn't sound the same. Also, much of the artwork's detail is lost on small CD inserts. If you don't know what I'm talking about, compare the wonderful details of the Beatles' *Sgt. Pepper's Lonely Hearts Club Band* album cover with the CD insert.

(A) My uncle has a very extensive record collection.
(B) Record enthusiasts flock to the annual record convention downtown.
(C) The recording industry should go back to the days of the vinyl album.

C. Exploring Language

Persuasive Writing Read the following persuasive paragraph. Write the letters of the two sentences that do *not* belong because they are based on the opinion of someone who is not an expert.

(A) Our school should abolish the rule requiring us to wear uniforms. (B) My brother says doing so will result in higher test scores because we wouldn't be so distracted by the hideous green-and-blue shirts. (C) If our school was to do away with uniforms, it would likely foster an atmosphere more conducive to creativity and personal expression, which are important to kids. (D) Also I recently read a study from the *Journal of Education Research* that stated uniforms actually have a negative effect on student academic achievement. (E) My parents both think it's ridiculous that we should be forced to wear these drab, uninteresting clothes every day. (F) If Avondale Creek School is truly interested in increasing our academic achievement, I urge the administrators to read research that addresses both sides of the school-uniform debate.

D. Expressing Yourself

Choose one of these activities. When you are finished, give your paper to your teacher.

1. Pretend your family owns a large farm and a neighbor wants to go hunting on it. Write a persuasive paragraph urging your parents to either allow the neighbor to hunt on their property or to forbid the neighbor from doing so. Make sure your claim is clearly stated and that you end with a strong closing sentence.

2. WORK with a PARTNER Work with a partner, and think about something you'd like to change at your school. It might be a dress code policy or a rule regarding the use of computers or cell phones. Discuss how you both feel about the policy or rule, and then write a claim or a topic sentence. Then write a persuasive paragraph that includes evidence to support your claim. Organize your arguments so they are in order from weakest to strongest. End with an appropriate closing sentence.

Unit 8

Expository Paragraphs

Topic Sentences

An **expository paragraph** gives information. It can tell facts, explain how to do something, or summarize a piece of writing. The **topic sentence** of an expository paragraph should help the reader understand the purpose of the paragraph. It can also contain the paragraph's claim or main idea. A topic sentence can come at the beginning or at the end of the paragraph.

What is the best topic sentence for each expository paragraph?

1. "The seven seas" is a figurative expression that refers to all the oceans and seas of the world. Some say that the seven seas are the North and South Atlantic, the North and South Pacific, the Indian, the Arctic, and the Antarctic Oceans. Others believe that the seven seas are the Atlantic, the Pacific, the Arctic, and the Indian Oceans as well as the Mediterranean Sea, the Caribbean Sea, and the Gulf of Mexico. Still another view is that the seven seas include the Mediterranean, Black, Red, Caspian, and Adriatic Seas as well as the Persian Gulf and the Indian Ocean. ______

(A) The world's seas and oceans contain a wide variety of life and remain among the last unexplored areas.

(B) There are more than seven seas in the world, not to mention the oceans.

(C) Clearly, there is disagreement over which seven bodies of water originally made up the seven seas.

---

2. A *shoecabbage* is not something you wear on your feet, nor is it a type of vegetable. ______ For example, "eye" is a shoecabbage because the Scots' meaning of this pronunciation is "yes." In Korean, the sound "pea" means "rain" or "broom." In German, the shoecabbage "lime" actually means "glue." How did this strange word come into existence? The word *chou,* pronounced like *shoe,* is the French expression for "cabbage."

(A) After more than twenty years of collecting examples of these words, Teresa Dowlatshahi coined the word *shoecabbage.*

(B) A *shoecabbage* is a word in a language other than English that sounds the same as an English word but has a completely different meaning.

(C) New words are continually being added to the English language as the need for them arises.

3. _____ First, choose a site that provides protection from the wind, such as an area next to a line of evergreen trees. At the same time, make sure that you do not set up your tent under branches that are loaded with snow. Second, do not choose a site on or at the bottom of a slope; such places may be susceptible to avalanches. Also, avoid camping in low valleys where the settling of cold air will make your camp uncomfortably chilly. Finally, try to choose a site near running water so that you won't have to waste precious fuel to melt snow.

(A) If you are selecting a site to set up a winter camp, keep these important points in mind.

(B) Winter camping can be a wonderful experience if you don't mind the cold weather and snow.

(C) You can use your skis and ski poles as tent stakes to reduce the amount of gear that you have to carry.

---

4. If you get a parakeet for a pet, the first thing to do is set up its cage. Ideally, you should provide two perches and a swing, as well as a few bells and colorful toys. Line the bottom of the cage with paper towels or newspapers, and attach plastic seed and water trays to the bars of the cage. Give the parakeet fresh food and water every day, and change the lining of the cage every three days. Once the parakeet has a comfortable home, you can teach it to perch on your finger and say a few simple words. _____

(A) Parakeets can be wonderful pets when they receive proper care and training.

(B) Parakeets are easier to take care of than parrots or other larger birds.

(C) Yes, parakeets can be taught to talk.

---

5. _____ The Chinese New Year begins with the first full moon of the year, which can be anywhere from late January to mid-February. Preparations for the holiday begin several days before the new moon. People clean their houses and decorate their doorways with red paper covered with symbols of good luck and praise of nature. On the eve of the New Year, families get together for a large dinner. The next fifteen days are a time of visiting relatives and paying respect to ancestors and nature.

(A) According to tradition, visitors give a bag of oranges and tangerines to their hosts.

(B) On the second day of the celebration, people make a point of being kind to dogs.

(C) The oldest and most important holiday in China, the New Year, is celebrated over a period of fifteen days and ends with the Lantern Festival.

Unit 9

Expository Paragraphs

Facts and Details

In an expository paragraph, **facts** and **details** are sentences that give information on the topic. They should support any claims you make. All the details in a paragraph must relate to the topic of the paragraph. Leave out anything unrelated to the topic or claim.

Choose the fact or detail that does *not* belong in each expository paragraph.

1. **(A)** To make a place setting for dinner, center the dinner plate on the table in front of the chair, and put the napkin on the plate. **(B)** Place the fork to the left of the plate. The bread plate goes above the fork. To the right of the plate, place the knife with the blade facing inward. **(C)** Ceramic plates are available in a variety of colors and styles. The spoon goes on the outside of the knife. **(D)** The glass goes on the right, near the top of the knife and spoon.

2. Throughout the world, the Statue of Liberty is the most recognized symbol of the United States. **(A)** The statue, however, was not built in the United States by Americans but was given to the American people by the French. **(B)** The Eiffel Tower is one of the most widely recognized symbols of France. When the Civil War ended, a French politician suggested a joint French-American monument to celebrate the ideal of liberty. **(C)** In 1871, French sculptor Frederic Auguste Bartholdi was chosen to build the statue. The original intention was to have the statue in place as a gift for the centennial celebration of the United States. **(D)** Problems with construction of the statue's base delayed the completion of the monument until 1886.

3. Nearly everyone is familiar with rainbows, but have you ever heard of a moonbow? **(A)** Rainbows are quite a sight to behold. **(B)** A moonbow is a nocturnal version of a rainbow. A moonbow forms when the light from a full moon shines on the mist of a waterfall. **(C)** When the moonlight shines at just the right angle on the droplets of water in the mist, they refract the light just like a prism does. **(D)** The effect created by this refraction is a faint band of colors arching across the waterfall.

4. **(A)** Making a simple compost pile is an environmentally friendly way to enrich soil and reduce waste. First choose a site for the compost pile that is downwind from your house. **(B)** Enclose the site with chicken wire, and cover the ground with soil. Use the compost pile to regularly dispose of kitchen wastes such as fruit and vegetable skins, eggshells, coffee grounds, tea bags, and used paper napkins. **(C)** Continue to add soil to the waste materials in the pile. Use a shovel or a pitchfork to turn the material over every day or two. **(D)** You can use the same shovel to dig holes for a garden. Spread the finished compost from the bottom of the pile around trees and plants in your garden.

---

5. **(A)** Are you tired of the same old boring lunchmeat and cheese sandwiches? A tuna salad sandwich is a delicious snack that's quick and easy to make. **(B)** First, open a can of tuna, and drain the water or oil from the can. **(C)** Albacore is a major source of canned tuna. Chop up some celery into small pieces. **(D)** Mix the tuna, celery, and some mayonnaise in a bowl. Spread the mixture on a slice of your favorite bread, and top it with another slice. Then enjoy your tasty new sandwich!

---

6. The folktale "The Gold Coin" was written by Alma Flor Ada. **(A)** It is about a thief named Juan. He works at night and has no friends or relatives. One night, peering through a crack in a hut, Juan sees Doña Josefa, the local healer, holding a golden coin in her hand. **(B)** Gold is one of the most valuable metals in the world. He decides to steal the woman's gold. Before he can carry out his plan, Josefa and her gold depart on a long journey to help a sick grandfather. **(C)** Juan sets out after her, but the clever medicine woman always stays one step ahead of him as she visits one sick person after another. **(D)** Eventually, Juan catches up to Josefa who gives him the coin. In the end, Juan does an act of kindness by giving the coin back to Josefa to give to someone who will need it more than he.

Unit 9
Expository Paragraphs

Choose the fact or detail that does *not* belong in each expository paragraph.

7. Lemurs resemble primitive primates that lived long ago. **(A)** Monkeys are often one of the most popular attractions at zoos. Today, these gentle, social creatures live in trees or in large bushes. They eat mainly fruits and insects, but some are more carnivorous than others. **(B)** Most lemurs are active during the day, while only the smaller species of lemurs, such as the pygmy mouse lemur, are active at night. They are also the least-recognized species of primates, although they have certain features that are particular to primates, such as grasping hands. **(C)** Unlike most primates, however, lemurs have a *rhinarium*—a moist, very sensitive nose. **(D)** Many also have tails, but they cannot hang from them like some primates can.

8. **(A)** Have you ever thought about how much we rely on batteries? Without them, much transportation would come to a grinding halt. **(B)** Lead-acid batteries either start or power cars, trucks, buses, boats, trains, and electric wheelchairs all over the world. **(C)** Sometimes batteries are able to be recharged. They also power electric forklift trucks used in warehouses, factories, mines, and ships. **(D)** Lead-acid batteries also keep the electric people-movers going in airports, as well as golf carts. On the road, these kinds of batteries power electric police vehicles, buses, and mail carrier vans.

9. **(A)** Before passage of the Federal Reserve Act in December 1913, local banks often didn't have the necessary funds to make reliable loans to businesspeople and farmers. **(B)** For want of adequate funds, stores and factories closed, and crops rotted. The Federal Reserve Act greatly improved this situation by providing for a new form of "flexible" currency known as Federal Reserve notes. **(C)** The new money went into circulation when local banks needing cash brought people's promissory notes to Federal Reserve Banks. **(D)** In its early days, the Federal Reserve System served as the nation's central bank. In return, the Federal Reserve Bank issued Federal Reserve notes, assessing the member bank a small fee called a *rediscount.*

10. With the high rate of travel among countries, the threat of worldwide epidemics is real. **(A)** Disease can spread more quickly than ever before. An outbreak of a disease in any part of the world can reach your state in a matter of days. **(B)** People often run a high temperature when they are sick. **(C)** Sometimes, diseases don't make people sick right away. People can be infected but not show any symptoms. **(D)** By the time they have symptoms or feel sick, they may have already infected other people. These others then go through the same cycles. Scientists and doctors want a better warning and surveillance program for these kinds of diseases.

---

11. **(A)** A butterfly begins its life in an egg and is known as a *larva* once it hatches from the egg. As the tiny larva, or caterpillar, eats, it grows bigger. Caterpillars eat a tremendous amount of food. **(B)** The larva then attaches itself to a twig and forms a hard outer shell called a *pupa.* Inside the pupa, or *chrysalis,* the caterpillar turns into a butterfly. After some time, an adult butterfly emerges from the chrysalis. **(C)** Some monarch butterflies migrate as far south as Mexico. Adult butterflies usually do not live for a very long time. **(D)** They cannot eat, but they drink nectar through a long, straw-like instrument called a *proboscis.* The adult female butterfly lays a fertilized egg, and the process begins again.

---

12. Everyone uses the same air that circulates around the planet. **(A)** Human activity increases the amounts of carbon dioxide, nitrous oxide, and methane in the atmosphere. **(B)** When people burn fossil fuels such as gas, coal, and oil, these chemicals pollute the air. **(C)** Carbon dioxide allows sunlight to get through, but traps heat radiated back up from Earth. This is the *greenhouse effect.* It functions the same way as glass in a greenhouse does. **(D)** Greenhouses typically protect plants from frost or freezing. The energy from the sun can penetrate through the atmosphere, but the heat radiated from Earth cannot. The heat remains trapped inside the atmosphere. The greenhouse effect may cause temperatures on Earth to get warmer.

Unit 10

Expository Paragraphs

Closing Sentences

An effective ending is one important feature of an expository paragraph. The **closing sentence** of an expository paragraph will often summarize the main idea. If the paragraph gives steps to complete a process, the closing sentence may give the last step in the process. It may also serve as a transition to the next paragraph. If nothing else, the closing sentence should make it clear to the reader that the paragraph is ending. For example, don't end a paragraph in the middle of a thought. Doing so could leave the reader confused, and your message will be lost.

Which closing sentence belongs at the end of each expository paragraph?

1. Washing a car is not very hard and can even be enjoyable on a hot summer day. First, fill a bucket with soap and water, and then soak a soft sponge in the bucket. Second, rinse off one side of the car with a hose. Make sure to get every part of that side of the car wet. Then start by washing the hood of the car, using a circular motion, and then move toward the trunk. It is important to rinse off all the soap before it dries. Repeat the same procedure on the other side of the car, making sure to rinse off all the water. ______

   (A) The next thing you know, you'll probably want to go for a spin in the nice, shiny, clean car!

   (B) Lastly, you should use a chamois to dry the car so there won't be any spots from dried water.

   (C) There are all different kinds of soaps from which you can choose.

---

2. It's true that men are credited with many inventions: light bulbs, assembly lines, and so on. Although you don't hear as often about women inventors, they do exist. In fact, you're probably sitting at the fruits of one woman's labors right now, and you have Anna Breadin to thank for it. She invented the school desk in Philadelphia, Pennsylvania, in 1889. Two years earlier in 1887, Maria Allen invented diapers in Brooklyn, New York. Before that, Sophia Steelman invented the washing machine at Somers Point, New Jersey, in 1883. These are only a few examples. ______

   (A) There have been many inventions credited to women that have made our world a better place to live.

   (B) I wonder if a man invented the outdoor grill.

   (C) Eli Whitney sought to profit financially from his invention of the cotton gin.

3. How did the constellations get their names? To people living long ago, arrangements of stars formed pictures in the sky. Pegasus, with its square body, long neck, and outstretched legs, reminded the Greeks of their mythological winged horse of the same name. Perseus and Orion reminded them of two of their heroes. Across the night sky with outstretched wings flies Cygnus. This constellation gets its name from the Greek word *kyknos,* which means "swan." Renaissance astronomers gave other constellations less poetic names. Here in the northern hemisphere is Triangulum, "triangle." In the southern hemisphere, you can look up and locate Telescopium, "telescope," and Microscopian, "microscope." ______

(A) A number of the constellations have been named after animals or mythological characters.

(B) Many stars can be seen on a clear night when you are far away from the glare of city lights.

(C) This is how some of the constellations got their names over time.

---

4. The subjects of American colonial literature were as diverse as the people who settled in America. Some colonial literature had religious themes. *The New England Primer,* for example, was a children's textbook that used religious instruction to teach reading, writing, and arithmetic. Among the most famous literature from this period was a sermon called *Sinners in the Hands of an Angry God* by Jonathan Edwards. Edwards wrote his sermon to persuade colonialists to take on the religious commitment that the first Puritan settlers had. His congregation was very moved when they heard this passionate sermon. ______

(A) Some writers were also moved by the injustice of slavery.

(B) Students who read colonial literature today can imagine themselves living in these interesting times.

(C) Reenactments of this period in American history give us a picture of what life was like back then.

---

5. The process of making orange juice begins in the field. Oranges are picked in groves and are then sent to a fruit processing center. Next, the fruit is washed with soap and water before being inspected. Then the oranges are passed through a machine that squeezes the juice out of them. Sometimes juices of different kinds of oranges are blended together. After that, the juice is then pasteurized to make sure it is safe to drink. The juice is then put into cartons, plastic jugs, or glass containers. ______

(A) Finally, the juice is distributed to stores throughout the United States and sometimes across the globe.

(B) Orange juice contains high amounts of vitamin C.

(C) Many people drink orange juice for breakfast every morning.

Unit 11

Writing Paragraphs

Descriptive Writing

Descriptive writing provides the reader with a clear, vivid picture of something or someone. When you include details in your writing, such as how something looks, smells, feels, tastes, or sounds, you can help the reader feel like he or she is part of the story or the scene. One way to organize details in a description is to tell them from left to right or right to left.

The old treasure box, filled with bright gleaming gold, lay open on the dank, chilly ground next to the bronze statue.

Do the paragraphs below have their descriptive details organized from left to right?

1. I absolutely could not wait to sink my teeth into the delicious frozen-yogurt sundae set before me. On the very top lay a bright red cherry—it didn't stay there for long! Below that, a layer of sweet whipped cream rested atop a heaping scoop of soft, velvety vanilla frozen yogurt, which sat in the middle of a pool of strawberry topping. That was my favorite part. Under the cup was a pile of napkins. They came in handy because it wasn't long before some strawberry sauce dripped from the spoon onto my brand new T-shirt!

(A) Yes.

(B) No, the details are organized from top to bottom.

---

2. Julio's room was a mess when he got home from baseball practice. Surveying the scene from his doorway, he knew he had his work cut out for him. On his bed was a pile of clothes that he had forgotten to put away before he left. Next to the bed was his desk, covered with his books and papers from the homework he did last night. He hadn't put them back in his backpack yet. To the right of the desk hung the shelf his uncle had built for him for his birthday last week. His model-car collection was disorganized. Some cars were even missing. Julio figured he'd have a talk with his little brother about that. For now, though, he sighed and began picking up the clothes off his bed.

(A) Yes.

(B) No, the details are organized from top to bottom.

3. Hockey is a fun game to watch. It moves fast and there is usually a lot of excitement. Have you ever seen a hockey rink up close? At one end of the rink is a goal net. The point of the game is to get the puck in your opponent's net past the goaltender. There are also different lines. The first line past the net is the blue line. To the right of the blue line is the center circle with a line drawn through it that divides the entire rink into two equal halves. After the center circle is another blue line. To the right of that blue line is the other team's net.
(A) Yes
(B) No, the details are organized from top to bottom.

---

4. It was early in the morning when Winona shuffled into her office. After getting her morning cup of coffee, she sat down at her desk as usual and prepared to finish her report for the meeting she was to hold next week. She put her disk into the floppy drive just as the monitor flickered on. Next to the monitor, the fan kicked on in the CPU as if to say "good morning." The printer to the right of the CPU came to life with a series of beeps—another greeting she looked forward to hearing every morning. Everything was going just fine until she looked at the calendar hanging next to her printer and realized that today was Saturday, not Friday!
(A) Yes
(B) No, the details are organized from top to bottom.

---

5. I wish you could have been with me this evening to watch the sunset on the beach. It was one of the most beautiful things I've ever seen in my life. The sky above the sun was deep purple, and the farther down you looked, the brighter the sky got until it turned orange. Just as the sun starting sinking into the ocean, it turned a shade of bright yellow. It looked as if it were actually sinking into the ocean! The water reflected this wonderful display of color in glorious shades of purple, orange, red, and yellow. The waves continued to roll in and hit my feet, washing away the sand from between my toes.
(A) Yes
(B) No, the details are organized from top to bottom.

Unit 11

Writing Paragraphs

Most of the time, descriptive writing appears as part of another form of writing, such as narrative, persuasive, or expository. The details of the descriptions help to keep the reader involved in the writing by making objects clearer in the readers' minds.

6. Which paragraph would most likely be the descriptive part of an expository essay?

(A) A platypus has a long, toothless snout that resembles a duck's bill. Also like a duck, a platypus has flat, webbed feet well-suited for swimming. Although a platypus is much larger than a mole, it has a similarly shaped stocky, tube-like body that is ideal for burrowing in the ground. A platypus is a mammal; however, it lays eggs, like birds and reptiles, instead of giving birth to live young. This mixture of features of different animals is what makes the platypus so unusual.

(B) The platypus is native to Australia and spends much of its time in freshwater streams and ponds. What is so strange about the platypus is that it is a mammal that lays eggs. After the eggs hatch, the young drink milk from tiny openings on their mother's stomach. A platypus usually lives for about ten to seventeen years.

---

7. Which paragraph would most likely be the descriptive part of a narrative essay?

(A) We walked along the gorge's edge looking for an entrance into the cave that would lead to the buried treasure. The map led us to this point, but we couldn't tell where to go from there. Kevin thought that the grove of palm trees below us might be a clue. I still wasn't sure. If we could only find the missing piece of the map, we would know for sure.

(B) Branson, Kevin, and I slowly made our way down the dark, damp, musty corridor. Firelight from small torches mounted on the wall helped to lead the way. It wasn't much light, but at least it helped. We could hear water dripping from somewhere; however, the sound echoed throughout the cavern, so it was hard to pinpoint exactly where it was coming from. All of a sudden we felt a cold breeze blow through our hair.

8. Which paragraph would most likely be the descriptive part of a persuasive essay?

(A) Before you decide to get a pet, think about the responsibilities involved with each kind of animal. When people take an animal as a pet, that animal largely depends on its owner for everything. A dog cannot feed itself or fill its bowl with water. On a similar note, a cat cannot clean its own litter box. Having a pet is great fun, but it is also a great responsibility that should be taken very seriously. Our pets' health and lives depend on it.

(B) I urge you to think carefully before you choose a pet. For example, do you really want to leave the cozy warmth of your home to walk a dog during cold, blustery winter evenings? Do you think you would enjoy cleaning a cat's litter box every day? I know that putrid smell is more than I can bear. Perhaps you should consider fish instead. Fish come in all kinds of bright and beautiful colors and interesting shapes. They are also easy to care for. Once you set up the tank, you need to clean it every two to three weeks only. The fish need to be fed only once a day.

9. Which paragraph would most likely be the descriptive part of an expository essay?

(A) Red Square in Moscow, Russia, is one of the most interesting places I've ever visited. First of all, it is home to one of the most beautiful cathedrals in the world. Saint Basil's Cathedral looks like something out of a fairy tale with its multicolored, onion-shaped domes. You really have to see it to believe it. Also in Red Square is the tomb of Vladimir Lenin, a leader of the Communist revolution. People form long lines to walk through this small marble structure to see Lenin's preserved body.

(B) There is much history contained within the walls of Red Square. During Soviet times, many military parades were held there. There are many famous buildings in and around Red Square, such as Saint Basil's Cathedral, Lenin's Tomb, the State Historical Museum, and a large shopping mall. Adjacent to Red Square is the Kremlin, which is the heart of the Russian government. Many foreign and Russian tourists visit this magnificent landmark every year.

The Third LAP
Language Activity Pages

A. Exercising Your Skill

You have been learning about topic sentences, facts and details, and closing sentences associated with expository paragraphs. You have also been learning about descriptive writing. Answer these questions about what you have learned.

1. What does expository writing do?
   (A) convinces the reader to think or feel in a certain way
   (B) tells a story
   (C) gives information, tells facts, explains how to do something, or summarizes a piece of writing

2. What does the topic sentence of an expository paragraph do?
   (A) helps the reader understand the purpose of the paragraph; it can also contain the paragraph's claim or main idea
   (B) brings the paragraph to a conclusion
   (C) introduces a new thought or idea

3. When is it okay for facts and details to stray away from the main idea of an expository paragraph?
   (A) if the facts and details are interesting or funny
   (B) it is never okay for facts and details to be off the topic
   (C) when the facts contradict something you stated earlier in the paragraph

4. What is one way to use a closing sentence in an expository paragraph?
   (A) to describe something
   (B) to introduce a new idea
   (C) to summarize the main idea

B. Expanding Your Skill

Number your paper from 1 to 2. Choose the descriptive sentence that has details organized from left to right.

1. **(A)** The bright-blue and yellow fish do nothing but swim back and forth all day.
   (B) Inside the aquarium lies a cluster of fluttering green plants next to a red bubbling castle.
   (C) Their food is on the second shelf below the net and cleaning supplies.

2. **(A)** On the table lay a knife and a fork beside a hot, steaming bowl of scrumptious, cheesy chili that is set next to a pile of napkins.
   (B) Below the golden cheese is a layer of spicy chili sauce, which lies atop a mound of fresh spaghetti noodles.
   (C) The wonderful smell is too much for me to bear—I'm going in for my first bite!

C. Exploring Language

Expository Writing Number your paper from 1 to 5. Read the topic sentence and the facts and details below it. Then write the letters of the five facts and details that you would include in a paragraph with that topic sentence.

A lobster is an ocean animal with a soft body protected by a rigid outer skeleton.

(A) Maine accounts for more than half of the lobsters harvested worldwide.

(B) The light, sweet meat of a lobster is considered a delicacy by many people.

(C) Its eight long, jointed legs project from the sides of its body, while two pairs of antennae stick out from the front of its head.

(D) Egg-bearing female lobsters that are caught in traps must be released according to federal law.

(E) A pair of powerful pincers, one larger than the other, protrudes from the front of a lobster's body.

(F) Like crabs and shrimp, lobsters are crustaceans.

(G) The lobster's muscular tail curls under at the end of its body.

(H) If a lobster is frightened, it uses its strong tail to propel itself backwards.

D. Expressing Yourself

Choose one of these activities. When you are finished, give your paper to your teacher.

1. WORK with a PARTNER Choose a partner. Think about how to get to a particular location within the school grounds, such as the library or the cafeteria. Without naming the location, write the directions on a sheet of paper. Make sure the directions are in the right order so that someone would be able to follow them. Then switch papers with your partner. Try to guess where the directions lead.

2. Use reference sources to find information about a popular tourist attraction in your state. Then imagine that you are on the visitor's council. Write a paragraph that gives information about the attraction. You may want to use such facts as when the attraction is open and why it is popular. Also include a description of the attraction so that someone who has never seen it may be able to picture it in their minds.

Unit 12

Writing Paragraphs

Staying on Topic

It is important for sentences in a paragraph, no matter if it is narrative, persuasive, or expository, to **stay on topic.** All of the sentences should provide information that supports the topic sentence if the paragraph has a topic sentence. Sentences that don't relate to the topic sentence or the main idea do not belong in the paragraph and should be taken out.

Which sentence in each paragraph does *not* stay on topic?

1. I am writing about a defective mobile phone that I recently got for my birthday. **(A)** The phone will not charge even when it is left on the charger for several hours. **(B)** The manager of the store where my dad bought the phone said that she could not exchange my phone for a new one. **(C)** The phone my parents gave me was turquoise; however, I think I would have liked a gray one better. **(D)** She said that the only way for me to get a new phone is to write directly to you, the manager of the company that distributes the phones.

2. J. K. Rowling, the author of the *Harry Potter* books, dreamed of being a writer but never thought that she would actually become one. **(A)** Rowling studied French rather than English literature at Exeter University. **(B)** After she graduated, she worked in various offices as a secretary for six years. **(C)** Then she took a job teaching English in Portugal. **(D)** As a child, Rowling had two friends named Ian and Vickie Potter.

3. I think the school cafeteria should change its menu in two ways. **(A)** First, the cafeteria should no longer serve pizza and hamburgers. **(B)** Some people like bacon on their pizza. **(C)** Students eat enough of these foods outside of school, and these foods are high in fat calories. **(D)** Second, the cafeteria should serve a greater variety of ethnic foods. Our school has many Hispanic and Asian American students who would appreciate seeing some familiar foods.

4. The next time you see a statue with a rider mounted on a horse, pay special attention to the position of the legs of the horse. **(A)** If both of the horse's front legs are raised in the air, this indicates that the person sitting on the horse died on the battlefield. **(B)** Although George Washington led many battles on horseback, he did not suffer fatal injuries. **(C)** If the person died a natural death, both of the horse's front legs will be on the ground. **(D)** If the person suffered wounds on the battlefield but died later, one of the horse's front legs will be raised in the air.

5. People in the United States should try to incorporate more walking into their daily routines. **(A)** Walking is good exercise, which many Americans don't get enough of. **(B)** Daily workout routines and team sports are other ways of exercising. **(C)** Walking is also a good way to clear one's mind after a long day of strenuous mental activity. **(D)** Through regular walks, a person can get to know his or her neighborhood and the people who live and work in the area.

6. Why do so many people from the Midwest and East Coast retire in Florida? **(A)** The most obvious reason, of course, is that the weather in Florida is much warmer throughout the year than the weather up north. **(B)** Another factor is the low humidity in Florida as opposed to dangerously high levels in northern summers. **(C)** Florida also has numerous condominiums—located on or near its many beaches—that are roomy enough for two people. **(D)** Still, many people who retire in Florida miss the changes of the seasons. Finally, so many people retire in Florida that it is easy for people of their age to make friends and enjoy active social lives.

7. A plantain looks like a large green banana. **(A)** Bananas are awesome when you cut one up and put it on certain kinds of cereal. **(B)** Although plantains are technically a type of tropical fruit, they are used more like a vegetable than a fruit and are cooked before being eaten. **(C)** In Hispanic and Caribbean cuisines, plantains are an everyday staple, much like a potato is in American cuisine. **(D)** Surprisingly, this interesting fruit also tastes very similar to a potato. They are delicious fried, baked, boiled, and served in soups and stews.

Unit 12
Writing Paragraphs

Which sentence in each paragraph does *not* stay on topic?

8. Padre Island is the largest undeveloped barrier island in the world. **(A)** Located off the southern coast of Texas along Madre Lagoon, Padre Island is administered by the U.S. National Park Service. **(B)** Texas is the second largest state in the United States. **(C)** The entire island is a recreational center and a wildlife preserve. **(D)** The Padre Island National Seashore includes more than 130,000 acres.

---

9. The idea of the distant lake sounded so wonderful that the young frogs, Morty and Furdy, could not stop thinking about it. **(A)** Everybody said that particular lake stretched out as far as the eye could see. **(B)** They had read about lush green rushes and tall grasses that line the edges of the lake. **(C)** The abundance of insects and small fish that supposedly populated the shallow water near the shore sounded like a dream to the two frogs. **(D)** Morty was a little plumper and greener than Furdy, although Furdy could croak louder. They agreed that they must make the journey to the lake together.

---

10. Have you ever wondered how social security numbers are assigned to people? **(A)** Inquiring minds think about a lot of things. **(B)** The first three numbers are based on the person's geographical location in the United States. **(C)** The other six numbers are randomly assigned. **(D)** The U.S. government so far has assigned more than 400 million social security numbers. No two people have the same social security number; even after a person dies, his or her social security number is not used again.

---

11. **(A)** Although Americans account for only five percent of the global population, we generate a staggering forty percent of the world's trash. **(B)** I wonder how much Afghanistan contributes to the world's population. **(C)** In fact, the average American is responsible for about 4.6 pounds of solid waste per day, which adds up to 1,460 pounds of garbage per year for every person in this country! **(D)** At this rate, Americans are producing trash faster than it can be broken down in nature or stored in landfills. Clearly, there is an urgent need for the citizens of this country to limit the amount of garbage they generate by recycling, reusing, and conserving resources.

Unit 12

Writing Paragraphs

12. Why does Swiss cheese have holes in it? **(A)** All cheeses are made with the use of various bacteria, which give different cheeses their distinctive flavors. **(B)** One of the three types of bacteria used in the production of Swiss cheese is *P. shermani.* **(C)** When this bacteria is added to the cheese mixture, it creates bubbles of carbon dioxide gas, which remain and become holes in the final cheese product. **(D)** Emmentaler is one of Switzerland's oldest cheeses and has a nutty-sweet, mellow flavor.

---

13. The spinner dolphin is known for its incredibly high leaps out of water. **(A)** These dolphins jump high into the air and completely spin their bodies up to seven times before diving back into the water. **(B)** Spinner dolphins sometimes travel in small groups, but they often swim together in pods of 200 or more. **(C)** They do not have a high survival rate in captivity. **(D)** They spend most of their time in the warm waters near Mexico, Hawaii, and Japan.

---

14. It's true that Mexican jumping beans do move, although they cannot actually jump like people can. They only rock back and forth or occasionally scoot a millimeter or two. The motion of the beans is caused by caterpillars that live inside them. **(A)** The caterpillars will metamorphose into butterflies in a few months. **(B)** When a caterpillar hatches from its egg, it burrows into the bean and eats the inside. **(C)** Then it builds a web along the inner wall of the bean. **(D)** When the caterpillar moves its body, it also moves the bean, causing it to "jump."

---

15. Frida Kahlo was a twentieth-century Mexican painter who expressed her many painful experiences in her art. **(A)** When Kahlo was six years old, she was stricken with polio, a disease that left her right leg withered and much weaker than the other. **(B)** While she was recovering, Kahlo began to paint. At the age of eighteen, Kahlo was involved in a serious bus accident and suffered a broken collarbone, broken ribs, a broken pelvis, a crushed right foot, and numerous fractures in her right leg. **(C)** During her long confinement in bed, Kahlo continued to produce paintings that expressed her suffering. **(D)** Art can be said to be an outward expression of inner thoughts and feelings.

Unit 13

Writing Paragraphs

Figurative Language

Figurative language is language that has a meaning beyond the actual meaning of the words. Figurative language is used to create vivid pictures in the reader's mind. Making comparisons is one form of figurative language. Two types of comparisons are similes and metaphors. You can use them in different kinds of paragraphs as an interesting way to describe something.

- A **simile** uses the word *like* or *as* to compare two different things. Similes can be used in a narrative, persuasive, or expository paragraph to compare two things as long as they fit with the topic.

  The police officer stood like a statue near the doors.

- A **metaphor** compares two different things without using the word *like* or *as*. It says that something *is* something. Metaphors are commonly used in the descriptive part of a piece of writing, such as poetry. They may also be used in narrative, persuasive, and expository paragraphs as long as they fit with the topic.

  The police officer was a statue standing near the doors.

Read the comparisons below to answer each of the following questions.

1. Which simile is more likely to be used in an expository paragraph?
   (A) History is like a mirror that reflects our past triumphs and defeats.
   (B) All my friends say my brother is like a clam because he always shuts himself in his room.

2. Which metaphor is more likely to be used in a narrative paragraph?
   (A) The car was a gently rocking hammock, and I slept deeply until we finally arrived home.
   (B) This photograph is a portal that takes you back in time and lets you see what life was like during the 1970s.

3. Which simile is more likely to be used in a persuasive paragraph?
   (A) My thumb pounded like a drum after I accidentally hit it with the hammer.
   (B) Our school is as precious as a jewel and should be treated as such.

4. Which metaphor is more likely to be used in an expository paragraph?
   (A) The frog prince was a locomotive running full steam ahead to make it into the castle before the drawbridge closed.
   (B) The story I read for this summary is a key to unlock the doors of your imagination and take you on an exciting journey.

Unit 13

Writing Paragraphs

Personification and exaggeration are two other types of figurative language.

- **Personification** is a figure of speech in which objects or ideas have human qualities. Personification is best used in narrative paragraphs or poetry. Do *not* use it in persuasive or expository paragraphs unless you are certain that it fits the topic.

  Smoke from the bonfire tickled my nose.

  The sun smiled as it rose to start the new day.

- **Exaggeration** is an overstatement of the truth. Writers use exaggeration to add humor or to emphasize a point in narrative or persuasive paragraphs. You should generally avoid using exaggeration in expository paragraphs because they are to be based on facts.

  Hector thought that if he could make it to the top of the hill, he could do anything.

  There is no better way in the world to spend your free time than volunteering at the local animal shelter.

Read the sentences below to answer each of the following questions.

5. Which example of personification is more likely to be used in a narrative paragraph?

   (A) The monitor may blink a couple of times when you first turn it on and should be considered normal.

   (B) The siren screamed as the police car raced to the scene of the accident.

6. Which example of exaggeration is more likely to be used in a persuasive paragraph?

   (A) This was the best day of my entire life—so far.

   (B) My mom's homemade chocolate pudding is the best dessert this side of Oklahoma has ever seen.

7. Which example of personification is more likely to be used in a persuasive paragraph?

   (A) Ernie's Energy Drink will give you a lift and help you get on your way each morning.

   (B) The change machine has eaten another dollar.

8. Which example of exaggeration is more likely to be used in a narrative paragraph?

   (A) Miss Gunterson is the best teacher in the world, and here are reasons stating why I think so.

   (B) Ben was so clumsy he couldn't walk a straight line for all the money in the world.

Unit 13

Writing Paragraphs

Word Choice

Choosing your words thoughtfully and carefully is always important no matter what you write. What kinds of words you use depend on whether you are writing a narrative paragraph, a persuasive paragraph, an expository paragraph, or a description. Different kinds of words work better for different kinds of paragraphs.

- When writing a narrative paragraph, use words that will move your story along. For example, if there is a lot of action in the story, use strong action verbs to show what the character is doing. Also, choose words in the dialogue that represent the way the characters would talk in real life.

  Pavel walked across the stage. ⟶ Pavel strutted proudly across the stage.

- When writing a persuasive paragraph, think about your audience, and use words that you think would affect them the most. To support your claim, choose words that appeal to your audience's emotions, logic, or both. A person's sense of logic is his or her understanding of what is factual and correct.

  We need a traffic light on our street to protect innocent children. (appeals to emotion)

  We need a traffic light on our street; in the past six months, fourteen accidents have occurred, involving thirty-one vehicles. (appeals to logic)

Read the sentences below to answer each of the following questions.

9. Which sentence from a narrative paragraph uses the strongest action verbs?

(A) I looked out the window, and a red pickup truck drove by.
(B) I stared out the window, and a red pickup truck went by.
(C) I stared out the window, and a red pickup truck whizzed by.

10. Which sentence from a persuasive paragraph includes words that appeal to an audience's emotions?

(A) Without your contribution, thousands of puppies will be homeless this holiday season.
(B) During the holidays, puppy and kitten sales increase by forty percent at local pet stores.
(C) January is always the busiest month at local animal shelters.

11. Which sentence from a narrative paragraph uses dialogue that best represents the way people actually talk?

(A) "Okay, kids, clear your desks because it's test time," said Mr. Phillips.
(B) "The time in which we are required to begin taking the test has descended upon us," said Mr. Phillips.
(C) "Come along now, children, and put your primers under your desks and prepare to begin your examinations," droned Mr. Phillips.

Unit 13

Writing Paragraphs

- When writing an expository paragraph, such as an explanation of a process, use time and order words correctly so that the different steps of the process are in the correct order. Also use exact words so the steps are clear and easy to follow.

  Empty the noodles into the pan. Stir in some spices. ⟶ First, empty the noodles into the pan. Next, add one teaspoon of the spices.

- When writing a description, use vivid adjectives and adverbs to describe what the subject looks like and how it moves and sounds. Don't go overboard with the describing words, or they will lose their effect with the readers.

  The icicles were long and sharp. ⟶ The icicles hung like gnarled fingers pointing toward the ground. (*not* The long, pointy icicles that were extremely sharp hung like twisted, gnarled fingers pointing coldly toward the hard, frozen ground.)

Read the sentences below to answer each of the following questions.

12. Which sentence from a description contains the most vivid adjectives and exact words?

(A) The long street contained pieces of garbage.
(B) Pieces of trash lay on the dirty street.
(C) Old newspapers and discarded boxes littered the abandoned alley.

---

13. Which sentence from an expository paragraph includes the most time and order words and exact words?

(A) Turn left at the light before you get to that one building.
(B) Turn left at the second light before you get to the gas station.
(C) Turn at the second light.

---

14. Which sentence from a description contains the most vivid adjectives and exact words?

(A) The hamburgers cooking on the grill gave off a nice smell.
(B) The aroma of cooked food came toward us from the grill.
(C) The delicious aroma of sizzling hamburgers wafted toward us from the grill.

---

15. Which sentence from a narrative paragraph includes the most vivid adjectives and adverbs?

(A) We were in the tent when we heard sounds from outside.
(B) As we huddled together in the cramped tent, we heard the snapping of twigs and the rustling of leaves.
(C) Huddled together in the tent, we heard something.

Unit 14
Writing Paragraphs

Transition Words

Transition words help connect your words and sentences clearly and smoothly. Transition words can indicate time, location, and order. They also can show cause-and-effect relationships and show comparisons and contrasts. Some transition words include the following:

next to	across from	next	after	later	finally
near	first	between	in back of	to the left of	

Which transition words best complete each paragraph?

New York City became the first capital of the United States (1) _____ the Constitution was ratified. (2) _____ a few years, the capital was temporarily moved to Philadelphia (3) _____ President George Washington decided on a permanent location. He (4) _____ chose a site along the Potomac River that included land from both Maryland and Virginia. In December of 1800, Washington, D.C., became the third and final capital of the United States.

1. **(A)** during **(B)** next **(C)** once
2. **(A)** During **(B)** Before **(C)** After
3. **(A)** after **(B)** while **(C)** because
4. **(A)** never **(B)** finally **(C)** between

The two different types of camels are the dromedary and the Bactrian. Dromedary camels have a single hump, (5) _____ Bactrian camels have two humps. Bactrians inhabit parts of Asia that experience frigid winters. (6) _____, these camels develop thick, shaggy coats to prepare themselves for the winter. (7) _____, dromedaries live in Africa, where temperatures are not nearly as cold. (8) _____, dromedary camels have relatively short hair. While both camels can survive in the extreme heat of the desert, only Bactrian camels can survive in long periods of temperatures below zero.

5. **(A)** whereas **(B)** just as **(C)** similarly
6. **(A)** Still **(B)** Nevertheless **(C)** As a result
7. **(A)** Similarly **(B)** Then **(C)** In contrast
8. **(A)** Finally **(B)** Therefore **(C)** Even so

Unit 14
Writing Paragraphs

Every year, my family and I go on a skiing trip to Colorado. On our trip last winter, I decided to try snowboarding. I thought I could learn to snowboard fairly quickly **(9)** _____ I was an experienced skier. **(10)** _____ I rented a snowboard and some boots, and then I rode the ski lift to a slope of medium difficulty. **(11)** _____ I started coasting down the slope, I fell into an awkward heap. Of course I got up and tried again, but my second attempt was also a failure. **(12)** _____, I realized that I should have taken a snowboarding lesson before attempting the slope on my own.

9.	**(A)** whereas	**(B)** although	**(C)** because
10.	**(A)** So	**(B)** Nevertheless	**(C)** Still
11.	**(A)** In back of	**(B)** As soon as	**(C)** Inside
12.	**(A)** Just in time	**(B)** Later	**(C)** First

Fallingwater is a breathtakingly beautiful house designed by architect Frank Lloyd Wright. Positioned **(13)** _____ a waterfall in the woods of Pennsylvania, Fallingwater is a perfect blend of modernism set in natural surroundings. The side of the house **(14)** _____ the waterfall is a series of rectangular sandstone levels projecting horizontally from a hill alongside the waterfall. **(15)** _____ the beige stone layers are broad bands of large windows opening onto decks. Anchoring all of these smooth stone layers is a base made of rough gray stones, which are also used in the columns that rise vertically **(16)** _____ the layers.

13.	**(A)** among	**(B)** between	**(C)** over
14.	**(A)** below	**(B)** in front of	**(C)** among
15.	**(A)** Beyond	**(B)** Between	**(C)** Far from
16.	**(A)** behind	**(B)** overhead	**(C)** in the distance

There are many benefits to landscaping a home by planting a variety of flowers, shrubs, and trees to attract birds. **(17)** _____ benefit of a good landscaping plan is that it will add to the beauty of the home's setting **(18)** _____ attract a variety of interesting birds. **(19)** _____ benefit of providing homes for birds is the fact that many birds eat insects that annoy humans. **(20)** _____, trees and shrubs arranged around a house can significantly lower heating and cooling costs.

17.	**(A)** Another	**(B)** Lastly	**(C)** The first
18.	**(A)** as well as	**(B)** nearby	**(C)** before
19.	**(A)** The first	**(B)** Another	**(C)** Later
20.	**(A)** Before	**(B)** Finally	**(C)** After

Unit 14
Writing Paragraphs

Which transition words best complete each paragraph?

(21) ______ the Brachiosaurus and the Allosaurus were both dinosaurs that lived at the same time, they were very different types of animals. The Brachiosaurus was a huge creature; it could grow to be 100 feet long and eighty tons in weight. (22) ______, an Allosaurus typically reached a length of only thirty feet and a weight of two tons. An Allosaurus was a two-legged meat-eater, (23) ______ a Brachiosaurus was a four-legged plant-eater. (24) ______ the Brachiosaurus, which was a solitary animal, the Allosaurus appears to have hunted in groups.

21. **(A)** Because	**(B)** Clearly	**(C)** Although
22. **(A)** Similarly	**(B)** In contrast	**(C)** Nevertheless
23. **(A)** just as	**(B)** unlike	**(C)** whereas
24. **(A)** Unlike	**(B)** Like	**(C)** Similar to

Motorists who run red lights may not get away with it even if there's no police officer around. Many cities today use red-light cameras, which provide all the evidence necessary to prosecute drivers who run red lights. Positioned at the tops of poles (25) ______ busy intersections, the cameras are focused (26) ______ toward the intersection. When a car goes through a red light, it triggers a mechanism on the roadway in the intersection. The trigger then sends a signal to the camera, which takes two photos of the car: first when the car is (27) ______ entering the intersection and (28) ______ another as the car reaches the middle of the intersection.

25. **(A)** beyond	**(B)** near	**(C)** under
26. **(A)** outside	**(B)** across	**(C)** inward
27. **(A)** just	**(B)** later	**(C)** far from
28. **(A)** then	**(B)** nearby	**(C)** first

Many people impulsively buy clothes, gadgets, and household items that they really don't need. (29) ______, people tend not to give these things away. (30) ______, numerous items simply end up unused in closets, basements, and garages. If this describes the situation (31) ______ your home, you might think about having a yard sale. (32) ______ helping you unclutter your home and reclaim your storage space, a yard sale can make money for you.

29. **(A)** In contrast	**(B)** Similarly	**(C)** At the same time
30. **(A)** As a result	**(B)** Nevertheless	**(C)** Similarly
31. **(A)** because	**(B)** inside	**(C)** whereas
32. **(A)** Before	**(B)** In addition to	**(C)** Unlike

Unit 14

Writing Paragraphs

Many kitchens are arranged in a similar way (33) _____ certain arrangements are most convenient for all users. (34) _____, the dishwasher is often installed just to the right of the sink. This allows people to rinse their dishes in the sink and load them in the dishwasher without having to walk any distance. (35) _____, people usually store glasses and dishes in cupboards above the dishwasher (36) _____ the dishwasher can be easily unloaded.

33. **(A)** because **(B)** as a result **(C)** nevertheless
34. **(A)** In addition **(B)** Similarly **(C)** For example
35. **(A)** In contrast **(B)** Behind **(C)** Similarly
36. **(A)** as soon as **(B)** so that **(C)** whereas

There are differences among meteors, meteorites, and meteoroids. (37) _____, meteoroids are small pieces that have broken off from comets but remain in the comet's original orbit. When a meteoroid (38) _____ nears Earth, it usually is burned up by Earth's atmosphere and, (39) _____, forms a glowing trail of gases. The meteoroid is called a meteor when this happens. Some meteoroids are large enough that they do not completely burn up when they enter Earth's atmosphere. (40) _____ a meteoroid strikes Earth's surface, it is known as a meteorite.

37. **(A)** Next to **(B)** First **(C)** Across
38. **(A)** onto **(B)** under **(C)** later
39. **(A)** as a result **(B)** in back of **(C)** to the left of
40. **(A)** After **(B)** Finally **(C)** Beyond

Have you ever noticed black or reddish marks on light-colored tiles in a shower? (41) _____, these marks are not dirt that no one has bothered to clean off. (42) _____, they probably are microscopic colonies of mildew: living organisms that are a type of fungus. Mildew spores are easily carried (43) _____ air and water. When a spore lands on even a particle of nutrient-rich dirt, it begins to grow into an entire colony if conditions are right. Mildew thrives in damp environments with temperatures (44) _____ about forty and ninety degrees. This is why mildew is common in showers.

41. **(A)** However **(B)** Therefore **(C)** More than likely
42. **(A)** In fact **(B)** Still **(C)** In addition
43. **(A)** across **(B)** over **(C)** through
44. **(A)** to the right **(B)** behind **(C)** between

Unit 15
Writing Paragraphs

Complete Paragraphs

A **complete paragraph** should have a topic sentence, details, and a closing sentence. All of the details should support the topic. The paragraph should include enough information to make your ideas clear and show connections between the sentences. If important information such as a detail or a closing sentence is missing, the paragraph will not make sense. Remember, however, that not all paragraphs, such as a narrative paragraph, need a topic sentence or a closing sentence. In this case, all the details should still support the topic of the paragraph.

Which sentence correctly completes each paragraph?

1. One of the definitions of the word *culture* is "the cultivation of living organisms." ______ For example, *agriculture* is the growing of crops and animals on land to be used for food, clothing, and shelter. *Horticulture* is a branch of agriculture that involves the cultivation of flowers and ornamental shrubs and trees. *Aquaculture* is the raising of aquatic animals and plants to be used as food.

(A) *Culture* can also be defined as a group of people's way of life.
(B) *Hydroponics* is the cultivation of plants using nutrient-filled water.
(C) Several specific types of cultivation include the root word *culture.*

---

2. The carambola is a tropical fruit that thrives in the Caribbean, South America, and Hawaii. It is a greenish-yellow, oblong fruit, three to five inches long, with five distinct ridges running lengthwise along its sides. ______ The fragrant flesh of a star fruit is also green-yellow and very juicy. The taste can range from exotically sweet to surprisingly tart.

(A) Another exotic fruit, the prickly pear, is also called a cactus pear.
(B) The fruit forms a star when cut in half, which is why it's also called star fruit.
(C) Would you try this fruit if you had the opportunity to do so?

---

3. ______ The whole atmosphere of the event was lively and spirited. Before the game started, crowds of enthusiastic fans wearing their team's colors streamed into the stadium and packed the stands. The game itself was just as exciting. The players were incredibly skillful and very tough physically. Both teams had numerous chances to score goals, but the goalkeepers for both teams kept making amazing saves. At the end of this thrilling game, the score was tied 1 to 1.

(A) When I'm old enough, I'm going to try out for the local soccer team.
(B) Baseball games are more fun to watch in person than on television.
(C) Last weekend I had a great time attending a Major League Soccer game for the first time in my life.

4. Covering almost half the continent of South America, Brazil is the fifth-largest country in the world. It includes more than 3.3 million square miles, including nearly 5,000 miles of coastline on the South Atlantic Ocean. ______ The interior of the country, which includes the Amazon Valley, is sparsely populated.

(A) I've been wondering if Brazil nuts actually come from Brazil, and if so, what part.
(B) Everyone should take a vacation in Rio de Janeiro at least once in their lives if it's possible.
(C) Despite its large area, much of Brazil's population is centered in its two largest cities: Sao Paulo and Rio de Janeiro.

---

5. Oregon's Crater Lake is one of the deepest lakes in North America. The lake was formed when an ancient volcano blew its top, leaving a massive crater that eventually filled with water. When you look out over the lake, the first thing you notice is a volcanic island in the middle of the lake. A flattened volcanic cone covered with vegetation rises from the island, called Wizard Island. The water surrounding the island is a deep, brilliant blue. ______

(A) Surrounding the lake is a rim of flattened cliffs that rise hundreds of feet above the lake.
(B) Lake Baikal in Russia is one of the biggest lakes in the world.
(C) The Great Lakes make up the largest freshwater system in the world.

---

6. ______ Snorkeling is more relaxing and peaceful than scuba diving, with the swimmer simply floating on the surface of the water and looking down into the underwater world below. Scuba diving requires much more energy than snorkeling and is more dangerous. However, it also allows people to dive to greater depths than snorkeling does to get a much better glimpse of organisms on the seafloor.

(A) I was so excited the first time I ever tried snorkeling while on vacation with my family.
(B) Snorkeling and scuba diving are different ways to view life under the surface of oceans and seas.
(C) Scuba is an acronym for "self-contained underwater breathing apparatus."

Which sentence correctly completes each paragraph?

7. A typical medieval feast for English royalty often consisted of three courses. Each diner began the meal with a loaf of bread and butter; a salad of mixed lettuces, herbs, and nuts; and a creamy apple or vegetable soup. The second course was typically centered around roast chicken, stewed beef, or roasted lamb. These meats were sometimes accompanied by carrots with honey, spinach and onions, and mushrooms cooked in broth. _____

(A) Hot honey lemonade was served at most medieval feasts.

(B) For the third course, medieval diners enjoyed spiced pears and oranges, as well as small seed cakes and wafers.

(C) Unfortunately, peasants were not so lucky.

---

8. Only very serious hikers even think about tackling the Appalachian Trail. The trail is a 2,167-mile-long footpath that traverses the ridges and valleys of the Appalachian Mountains. _____ Out of the several thousand people who begin the trail each year, only about three in twenty finish the entire hike. It takes between five and seven months for most hikers to make a complete trip.

(A) Many tips for successfully completing the hike are available from former hikers of the trail.

(B) The Appalachian Trail Conference is a volunteer organization that takes care of the trail.

(C) Crossing fourteen states, the trail begins in Maine and ends in Georgia.

---

9. The students in our school should be allowed to have a study period for the last half hour of every school day. _____ On the contrary, a study period would actually enhance learning. If we had time to study in school, we would have a chance to ask our teachers or other students for help with concepts that we don't understand. Also, many teachers assign a lot of homework, and a study period would really help us to get a good start on it every day.

(A) Some teachers might think that this would take valuable time away from learning.

(B) Also, we should not have homework assignments over the weekend.

(C) Many students belong to clubs or sports teams that meet right after school.

10. There is a specific name for different shades of all different kinds of colors. Crimson, vermilion, scarlet, burgundy, maroon, cardinal, ruby, and magenta are just some of the many shades of red. Sapphire, azure, ultramarine, teal, turquoise, and slate name different kinds of blues, while yellow can take the form of goldenrod, canary, or saffron. ____

(A) Different mixtures of blue and green create a wide range of shades.

(B) Brown can range from umber, sienna, russet, chestnut, and sepia, to taupe, khaki, tawny, tan, and beige.

(C) The names of many gems are also the names of colors.

---

11. If you have a few hours to spare each week, consider volunteering for the Meals on Wheels program. Meals on Wheels provides home delivery of nutritional meals for elderly people and others who are not able to cook for themselves. Many of these people would go hungry if not for this program. ____ Sometimes, the volunteer who delivers the meals is the only person a Meals on Wheels recipient sees all day long.

(A) Another benefit to volunteering your time is that most recipients will enjoy your company.

(B) During World War II, the first Meals on Wheels had its origins in Great Britain.

(C) Meals on Wheels delivers lunches and dinners nationwide.

---

12. When the explorer was still far from his destination, the clouds darkened, and rain began to pour down on him. Soon, he was soaking wet. He struggled along the path, barely able to see in the darkness and sometimes losing his footing on the slippery rocks. ____ From far within the cave, a blaze of light reached his eyes. For several moments, the explorer stood just inside the entranceway trying to make out the source of the light. This was no use, for the light was too distant. Finally, he began feeling his way along the wall of the cave toward the light.

(A) The explorer's greatest pleasure was taking long walks through the woods.

(B) Dripping with moisture, the explorer reached the ruins of an ancient castle.

(C) Dripping with moisture, the explorer at last came to the entrance of a cave.

The Last LAP

Language Activity Pages

A. Exercising Your Skill

You have been learning information about paragraphs that stay on topic, figurative language, word choice, transitions, and complete paragraphs. Answer these questions about what you have learned.

1. What is the difference between a simile and a metaphor?
   (A) A simile compares two things by saying that something is another thing, and a metaphor compares by using the word *like* or *as.*
   (B) A simile compares two objects, and a metaphor compares three or more objects.
   (C) A simile compares two things using the word *like* or *as,* and a metaphor compares by saying that something *is* another thing.

2. In which kinds of paragraphs is it necessary to stay on topic?
   (A) narrative and expository
   (B) persuasive only
   (C) narrative, persuasive, and expository

3. What kinds of words would be most effective for a persuasive paragraph?
   (A) words that appeal to either the reader's emotions or reason
   (B) words that will carry your story along
   (C) words that describe how an object looks, sounds, and moves

4. What do transition words do?
   (A) tell who is speaking in a narrative paragraph
   (B) introduce a new idea at the end of any kind of paragraph
   (C) help connect your words and sentences clearly and smoothly

B. Expanding Your Skill

Which word or words best complete each simile or metaphor?

1. When she plays the piano, my sister's hands are _____ flitting across the keys.
   (A) ants **(B)** butterflies **(C)** squirrels

2. The road down the mountain stretched before us as straight as _____.
   (A) an arrow **(B)** a branch **(C)** a fork

3. This sandwich is as soggy as _____!
   (A) a plastic bag **(B)** a rock **(C)** a wet noodle

4. The books were _____ weighing down my backpack.
   (A) a bag of sand **(B)** a basket of fruit **(C)** a can of soup

C. Exploring Language

Narrative Writing Read the words and phrases in the box. Number your paper from 1 to 12. Use what you have learned about word choice and figurative language to complete the paragraph by choosing words from the box to finish the sentences.

lead weight	as toothpicks	felt like I was far above Earth
collapsed	grueling	proudly raised its shoulders
magnificent	revived	sharp, craggy
taunted us	trek	absorbed

During our trip to the Rocky Mountains, we decided to make the long (1) _____ up the tallest mountain, which (2) _____ far above the others. Our hike up the (3) _____ slope took forever. Within a few hours, my legs became so tired that they felt as weak (4) _____. My backpack was a heavy (5) _____ weighing me down. The mountain (6) _____ with its enormous height and (7) _____ rocks. When we finally reached the peak, I was so exhausted that I (8) _____ onto the ground. After a few minutes, I (9) _____ myself and (10) _____ the (11) _____ view. I (12) _____, looking downward and across a land that had no end.

D. Expressing Yourself

Choose one of these activities. When you are finished, give your paper to your teacher.

1. WORK with a PARTNER With a partner, write a paragraph about a new invention. It may be any kind of invention—from a robot or a flying car to something that does not even exist yet. Tell what it is, what it does, and how it would help people. Include a simile or a metaphor and an exaggeration. Also make sure the paragraph stays on topic and is complete with a topic sentence, details, and a closing sentence.

2. Write a paragraph about nature in which you use descriptive words and at least one metaphor, simile, and example of personification.

PARAGRAPHS Scope and Sequence • *Specific Skill Series for Language Arts*

Unit/Level	Level A	Level B	Level C	Level D	Level E	Level F	Level G	Level H
Unit 1	Types of Paragraphs	Types of Paragraphs	Types of Paragraphs	Types of Paragraphs	Narrative Paragraphs	Narrative Paragraphs	Narrative Paragraphs	Narrative Paragraphs
Unit 2	Types of Paragraphs	Using a Web	Using a Web	Using a Web	Narrative Paragraphs	Narrative Paragraphs	Narrative Paragraphs	Narrative Paragraphs
Unit 3	Using a Web	Topic Sentences	Topic Sentences	Topic Sentences	Narrative Paragraphs	Narrative Paragraphs	Narrative Paragraphs	Narrative Paragraphs
Unit 4	Topic Sentences	Details	Details	Details	Narrative Paragraphs	Narrative Paragraphs	Narrative Paragraphs	Narrative Paragraphs
Unit 5	Topic Sentences	Closing Sentences	Closing Sentences	Closing Sentences	Persuasive Paragraphs	Persuasive Paragraphs	Persuasive Paragraphs	Persuasive Paragraphs
Unit 6	Details	Complete Paragraphs	Complete Paragraphs	Complete Paragraphs	Persuasive Paragraphs	Persuasive Paragraphs	Persuasive Paragraphs	Persuasive Paragraphs
Unit 7	Closing Sentences	Staying on Topic	Staying on Topic	Staying on Topic	Persuasive Paragraphs	Persuasive Paragraphs	Persuasive Paragraphs	Persuasive Paragraphs
Unit 8	Complete Paragraphs	Time and Order Words	Time and Order Words	Transition Words	Expository Paragraphs	Expository Paragraphs	Persuasive Paragraphs	Persuasive Paragraphs
Unit 9	Staying on Topic	Using Dialogue	Using Dialogue	Sentence Variety	Expository Paragraphs	Expository Paragraphs	Expository Paragraphs	Expository Paragraphs
Unit 10	Time and Order Words	Making Comparisons	Making Comparisons	Using Dialogue	Expository Paragraphs	Expository Paragraphs	Expository Paragraphs	Expository Paragraphs
Unit 11				Figurative Language	Writing Paragraphs	Writing Paragraphs	Expository Paragraphs	Expository Paragraphs
Unit 12					Writing Paragraphs	Writing Paragraphs	Writing Paragraphs	Writing Paragraphs
Unit 13					Writing Paragraphs	Writing Paragraphs	Writing Paragraphs	Writing Paragraphs
Unit 14					Writing Paragraphs	Writing Paragraphs	Writing Paragraphs	Writing Paragraphs
Unit 15					Writing Paragraphs	Writing Paragraphs	Writing Paragraphs	Writing Paragraphs
Unit 16							Writing Paragraphs	Writing Paragraphs